How to Fear God
Without Being Afraid of Him

The 1995 Chapel of the Air 50-Day Spiritual Adventure "Facing Down Our Fears"

Scared to Life, by Douglas J. Rumford. Discover how to break free of the gravitational pull of fear and its draining power by relying on God's resources. Book includes group discussion questions. Catalog no. 6-3413.

How to Fear God Without Being Afraid of Him, by David New and Randy Petersen. Do you have an unhealthy fear of God? This book will help you better understand God's power and holiness, balanced with His great love and care for each of His children. Catalog no. 6-3414. Audio book also available, Catalog no. 3-1228.

Adventure Journals. Dig deeper into the Adventure with day-by-day personal growth exercises. Available in the following editions:

Adult	Catalog no. 6-8870
Student	Catalog no. 6-8868
Children, grades 3–6	Catalog no. 6-8867
Critter County Activity Book (K–2)	Catalog no. 6-8866

ALSO AVAILABLE

Church Starter Kit	Catalog no. 6-8879
Children's Church Leader's Guide	Catalog no. 6-8865
Small Group Starter Kit	Catalog no. 6-8871
Student Leader's Guide	Catalog no. 6-8869

Contact your local Christian bookstore for still other 1995 Adventure products.

How to Fear God
Without Being Afraid of Him

David New and Randy Petersen

VICTOR BOOKS

A DIVISION OF SCRIPTURE PRESS PUBLICATIONS INC.
USA CANADA ENGLAND

Unless otherwise indicated, all Scripture quotations are from the Holy Bible, New International Version®. *Copyright © 1973, 1978, 1984 by International Bible Society. Used by permission of Zondervan Publishing House. All rights reserved. Other quotations are from the* New Revised Standard Version of the Bible (NRSVB), *copyrighted 1989 by the Division of Christian Education of the National Council of Churches of Christ in the United States of America, and are used by permission. All rights reserved.*

Copyediting: Barbara Williams
Cover Design: Scott Rattray
Cover Photo: SPG International; Jamie Herstein

Library of Congress Cataloging-in-Publication Data

New, R. David
    How to fear God without being afraid of him / by David New and Randy Petersen.
    p. cm.
    ISBN 1-56476-414-1
    1. God—Worship and love. 2. Fear of God. 3. Punishment—Religious aspects—Christianity.   I. Petersen, Randy.
    II. Title.
BV4817.N37 1995
231.7—dc20   94-29649
                                     CIP

Contents

Introduction

The little girl hid behind her teacher as I visited her Sunday School class. She peeked out and pointed at me, whispering, "There he is!"

"And who is that?" the teacher asked.

The three-year-old kept her gaze fixed on me. "God!" she said.

I stooped down and explained to the girl, and to the rest of the class, that I was not God, I was only the pastor. But the episode made me think. I wondered how many of the children of that church had created an image of God based on who I was and how I related to them. It was a sobering thought.

Many grownups, I believe, still have ideas about God that were based on authority figures in their past—parents, teachers, bosses, even pastors. Often these images are unduly harsh and demanding. They may have a thread of biblical truth, but they usually ignore the broad tapestry of God's love and forgiveness.

This book takes those harsh images head-on, contrasting them with the balanced teaching of Scripture. I hope that readers will find healing, comfort, and new intimacy with God as they read these pages.

In addition, we have included questions for reflection and/or discussion after every pair of chapters. We urge readers to talk through the issues raised by this book, or at least think through the implications for their own lives.

* * *

Coauthors David New and Randy Petersen have shared in the development of this book, though to avoid confusion, David's singular voice is used throughout. Many examples are used, from friendships to counseling sessions. Caught between the double values of confidentiality and journalistic integrity, we have chosen to change names and some minor details in some of the stories. The stories are true, but the identities are disguised.

We wish to thank our friends at Chapel of the Air for helping to create this book, especially Marian Oliver and David Mains.

David New
Randy Petersen

Chapter One

NEVER GOOD ENOUGH!

God as an Overcritical Teacher

Bobby was only eight years old, but already he had gotten himself into a lifetime's worth of trouble. His third-grade teacher refused to allow him in her class anymore, unless he received some counseling. So Bobby's mother brought him to see me. While the boy waited in the outer office, the mother filled me in on his background.

"I don't know what it is," she said, "but Bobby seems to be angry at everyone. He has no friends, at school or anywhere else. He argues with other children and bullies them. I have even seen him go out of his way to hurt another child."

I could see the pain in her eyes as she described the mysteriously bad behavior. She was at her wits' end. "It's funny," she said, "but he seems very concerned about fairness.

If we're cutting a birthday cake or something, he makes sure that his piece is just as big as everyone else's. But then he goes and treats other children so unfairly! I just don't understand him."

"How does he get along with the others within the family?" I asked.

"Well, he fights with his sister," she replied. "I guess a lot of little boys do that. With me, he's—well, he's a handful. Whenever I tell him to do something, he does exactly the opposite. And with my husband, his stepfather, Bobby just goes ballistic. Bobby's always angry at him, for no good reason. He doesn't even give him a chance."

It was time to talk with Bobby. The boy trudged into my office as if he were visiting a dentist. When he realized his mother would be leaving us, he became more talkative and relaxed. We spent the next half hour just getting acquainted. In the course of our conversation, I tried to get a sense of the different emotions this youngster had. At one point I asked, "Are you ever afraid?"

Bobby answered quickly, "No! I am not afraid!" Then after a brief pause, he looked away and said, "I do have a scary dream. I have it all the time."

"Would you tell me about it?" I asked.

For the next few minutes the boy shared with me his recurring dream—a dream that revolved around the flat-line signal and sustained beep of a heart monitor. It was that scene so often used on television and in movies to let the audience know the patient died. That image was fixed in Bobby's mind and haunted him frequently.

In later counseling sessions I heard more of Bobby's story. His behavior seemed more understandable in light of the horrible sequence of events in his young life.

Four years earlier, Bobby's father had left the home abruptly. Bobby had not seen him since. Coincidentally, the father had left the day after an accident that occurred while he and Bobby had been working on a backyard project. The father had cut his hand badly and had rushed off to the hospital. Bobby determined that the accident was his fault. In his young mind, it all fit together—the accident, his dad's departure, the divorce. Bobby blamed himself for it all. He wasn't sure what he had done, but he assumed he was responsible.

Soon after that, the family's small puppy was killed in front of the house. A quick replacement pet, a kitten, died only days later in Bobby's bed. Poor Bobby wondered if he were also responsible for these deaths.

To make matters significantly worse, his grandfather died within that same month. The one thing that stuck in his head at the funeral was the pastor's statement, "God has taken our dear brother home." The words were meant for comfort, but they had a chilling effect on this bright little four-year-old.

It was *God* who did all this. God took Grandfather, so God must have taken the cat and dog. And no doubt it was God who took Bobby's father away. As Bobby put it together, he felt God must be getting back at him for something terrible he had done. Only he wasn't sure what he had done wrong.

Everyone and everything that Bobby had loved left or died. And Bobby held himself responsible. He was now afraid to love, afraid that he would be hurt again. He was afraid of the flat line, the prolonged tone, those hospital signals that ushered his loved ones away from him. And so he steeled himself against those who cared about him the most.

At the close of one particularly tense session, I sensed Bobby's fear more strongly than ever. "You know," I said softly, "God loves you. He really cares about you. Maybe we could pray to God together and tell Him about some of these feelings."

Bobby immediately stiffened up. He stood up straight and loudly protested, "No, don't pray! I don't want you to pray. I don't want to talk to God!"

The sudden rage threw me. I wasn't sure what to say. But before I could respond, he added nervously, "God took away my grandpa and my puppy and my kitty . . . and my dad. I don't want to talk to God."

Here was a child who was confused, afraid,

and feeling very much alone. As Bobby saw it, God was mean and unfair, petty and vindictive. Instead of being a Comforter, God seemed to be a Tormentor. Bobby felt that he was being punished by God, but he didn't know what he was suffering *for*. What had he done to deserve all that? God had given everyone else the larger pieces of cake, but cheated Bobby out of his fair share. The boy learned that he would have to fight for whatever he got. Punish others before they punish you. Reject others before they reject you. Even if that means rejecting God.

Unfortunately, Bobby is not alone. Many people, old and young, are afraid of God. This feeling has nothing to do with the "fear of God" that Scripture promotes. Instead, it is based on a false impression of who God is, and how God feels about us.

Bobby saw God as a harsh authority figure, perhaps like an overcritical teacher he might have in school, one who punished him unfairly. His response was to avoid God entirely. Or try to. He didn't realize how much God loved him.

Visions of Wrath

When I was Bobby's age, I attended my first revival service. The experience would affect the way I thought about God for many years.

Each spring, an itinerant evangelist would come to our church and hold nightly services for at least a week, sometimes two. It was a time to invite friends and neighbors to hear the Gospel, though the crowd was mostly church people.

The evangelist that year was a large, burly man with cold, steely eyes. His voice was deep, almost hoarse. He had a way about him that commanded absolute attention. He certainly had mine.

The preacher trumpeted his warnings about the danger of hell and the damnation that faced the sinner. God would come with vengeance, he said, and at the most unexpected time. With his words, this man skillfully painted a picture of a vengeful and angry God. The longer he spoke, the more vivid the picture.

I snuggled close to my mother during the preacher's tirade. When he was finished and the service was dismissed, I breathed a sigh of relief. On the way home, I said nothing, though I was gripped with a fear that I had never known before.

It was soon bedtime. My little brother was already asleep and Mother was saying good night to me. As she left our room, she flipped the light switch off. The sudden darkness sent a chill through me. I sat up straight and nearly screamed my protest, "No, Mommy!" Then, more subdued, "Please, can we leave the light on for a little while? You can turn it off after I go to sleep." In truth, I had no intention of going to sleep that night.

With the light on again, my mother asked, "What's wrong, Honey?"

"Nothing," I said as bravely as I could.

She did not press me, but simply said, "OK," and promised to look in later.

As I lay in bed that night, I envisioned all the scenes the evangelist had painted earlier in his sermon—scenes of hell and a wrathful God coming quickly, like a thief in the night.

I didn't know exactly why, but I was sure I was a sinner and that I could not possibly survive the coming judgment. So intense was my fear of God that I insisted the light be left on. If He really did come that night, I wanted to see Him. I would not be caught in the dark. I trembled at the thought of God sending His angels in fearful wrath upon a sin-darkened world . . . my world.

That picture of God would haunt me for many years to come. I suppose it did keep me from doing many things I knew to be wrong. I certainly didn't want to bring judgment on myself. But this attitude also kept me from having any sense of joy about the Christian life. For a long time, it held me back from experiencing a deep love for my Lord.

The Beginning of Wisdom
The Bible calls the fear of the Lord "the beginning of wisdom" (Prov. 9:10). Indeed it is. Any reasonable grasp of reality must begin with an understanding that there is a divine

being stronger than we are, a God who cares about how we live—so we need to please Him. This is the proper starting point. As I said, my childhood fear of God kept me from some sins. I wasn't ready yet to reason out the morality of each forbidden act, I just knew that God said it was wrong (usually through my parents, His earthly representatives).

A friend of mine, a junior high teacher, told me how important it is to start the year being very strict. She has to instill fear in her students, or they won't learn a thing. After a few weeks of setting her standards, she can lighten up and really enjoy her students. But first they need to learn the behavior she expects, and they need to fear the consequences of crossing her.

It may be like that with God. We must start with the knowledge that He is Almighty, someone we must deal with. And we need to know what He wants from us.

But we must not stay at the point of fear. Scripture urges us to step into love. In a society browbeaten by legal restraints, Jesus summed up the Law as "Love the Lord your God with . . . [all of who you are]" (Matt. 22:37). Love, the Bible says later, is "the fulfillment of the Law" (Rom. 13:10). In his famous Love Chapter, the Apostle Paul said, "When I was a child, I talked . . . thought . . . reasoned like a child. When I became a man, I put childish ways behind me" (1 Cor. 13:11).

Does that mean we must toss out the fear of God entirely? Was that just part of the "childish" past? Should we scuttle it as we reach maturity?

These questions would be easy if we could say that the Old Testament is about fear and the New Testament about love. But that's not true. God extends His love throughout the Old Testament, and the idea of fearing God is present (though not as strong) in the New Testament.

Yet the Apostle John wrote, "There is no fear in love. But perfect love drives out fear, because fear has to do with punishment. The man who fears is not made perfect in love" (1 John 4:18). The word *perfect* in the original Greek of the New Testament carries the idea of maturity, completion. Within a life of mature Christian love, John is saying, we can have confidence in the face of God's judgment. We stand, by God's love, in the shoes of Christ. So there's no more need for our knees to knock. Our fear has grown up into love.

How do we put John's powerful statement together with other biblical texts promoting the fear of God? Well, it seems there are two parts of fear—the *regard* and the *distance*. First we understand the power and standards of the one we fear, then we stay as far away as possible.

Some of the Hebrew words for fear that were used in the Old Testament carry the idea of shrinking back or recoiling from the object of fear. That's the distance part. I find it interesting that, in the New Testament era, the Gentiles who were interested in Judaism were called "God-fearers." They had a regard for God's power and holiness, but being Gentiles, they kept their distance.

Yet the New Testament tells us that "you who were once far away have been brought near by the blood of Christ" (Eph. 2:13). It is the *distance* that is abolished by God's love. He reaches out to us and pulls us close. We retain a healthy *regard*—a "fear," if you want to call it that—of His power and righteousness. But we can relax a bit in the acceptance we find in Christ.

Trial and Terror

People often tell me about their childhood fear of God—not just a "beginning of wisdom" kind of fear, but an absolute terror. This terror has been cultivated by the teaching of parents or the preaching at church. It may be based on biblical truths about God's power and holiness, but it leaves out some other essential biblical ingredients—God's love and grace. That teaching does not divide the regard from the distance. Children learn that they are far, far from ever pleasing God.

This terror can cripple someone for life, spiritually speaking. People enter adulthood clinging to this image of God as an overcritical teacher, one who hunts down your mistakes and punishes you for them. As they see it, God is "out to get them" for every little sin. They are sure they can never fully measure up to God's standards, and that God is regularly disappointed in them. Forgiveness is a theological idea, but not an emotional assurance. They are sure God continues to hold their sins against them.

It's important to note that this "false image" of God is held by Christians and non-Christians alike. Many devout believers within the church are held back by these ideas. They could develop into mature, vivacious, powerful servants of God, but they're afraid.

We see this "fear of the overcritical teacher" in the following ideas. You may have heard some of these—or expressed them yourself.

God keeps a permanent record of my sin. I have heard people say that they feel limited in their relationship with God because of some sin they committed in the past. They feel they proved themselves unworthy with that past mistake, and God will never forget it.

God will punish me for every mistake I make. God is seen as a sort of Santa Claus, "checking to see who's naughty and nice." People imagine Him with a scorecard, tallying our few rights and our many wrongs.

If things are going badly, I am being punished for some sin. I remember a time when I was violently ill with the flu, back when I was a teenager. I confessed every sin I could think of. I was sure that God was "getting me" for something. Many people, including Job's friends (Job 4:7-8), have had the same idea.

I can never be loving enough to others, bold enough in sharing my faith, or humble enough in my own spirit. People have a standard of perfection, which is nice to shoot for, but they never make it. I have seen people do incredibly loving deeds and then chastise themselves for not doing more. They might invite the 7–11 clerk to church, but then feel guilty for not stopping into every other 7–11 in the tri-state area. Just once, I'd like to hear someone say, "By God's grace, I did a loving deed today, and I feel good about it." But then God might get you for being too proud.

Great Expectations

From her sickbed, Elsie, an elderly member of my church, told me her story. Her father was a pioneer preacher who had proclaimed the Word with exactness and enforced it with legalistic fervor. Elsie now spoke of him with kindness, but at one time she had despised him for the life he had forced on her, the other children, and their mother. She told me about the fear and guilt she had experienced as a young girl, seldom getting any words of love or approval from her father, and knowing she could never please the harsh and judgmental God he preached about. It seemed impossible to meet the expectations of either.

Elsie knew she would never be good enough to pass God's inspection. She feared she would never be allowed into God's heaven.

"Oh, my," she mused from the sickbed in her country home, "I was so afraid of him—my father. Yes, yes, and I was afraid of God. I just had all the wrong ideas about who God was." Elsie took a thoughtful pause and added, "Took me a long time to realize how good He was ... and that He really loved me."

Elsie took her concepts of God from her own father. I've counseled many adults—men and women alike—who are still trying to please their fathers or mothers, and finding it very difficult to do so. It seems we've had an epidemic of critical, demanding, and uncommunicative parenting in our world. And the children pay the price—all their lives.

It should not surprise us that many people see God as the same kind of parent—setting impossibly high standards and punishing us, or despising us, when we fail to meet them.

Results and Recovery

These ideas cause some people to *reject God*. In their minds, it's an act of self-preservation. If they can't win, they don't want to play God's game. This is sort of where little Bobby was, refusing even a simple prayer.

Other people with this false image of God

begin to *hate themselves*. They are very aware of their own sin, and they figure they will never be able to amount to anything.

Many, many Christians who fear God as an overcritical teacher just *never take risks*. They are like the servant in Jesus' parable who buried his money in the ground because he was afraid. These Christians are afraid that anything new, adventurous, creative, or never-been-done-before might be sinful. They tend to keep their own spiritual lives, and often their churches, in bondage to stale traditions.

And others are like me, the fretful boy. They *miss the joy and love of Christ*. Thankfully, His love and joy became very real to me later in life. But many Christians resign themselves to a fearful, tearful existence—always kneeling, never dancing.

In pop psychology these days, it's in vogue to talk about "healing the inner child." Many people who have had overcritical earthly parents or teachers are urged to deal with their childhood issues through confrontation or hypnosis or regression of some kind. I don't need to comment on those methods, but I would point out that many of our false images about God are planted during childhood. By now they may be deeply rooted.

We need to go back to the basics. Who is God? How does He feel about us? What does the Bible really say? We'll start to take some positive steps in the next chapter.

Chapter Two

HE KNOWS
WHAT WE
ARE MADE OF

God Understands, Cares, and Forgives

Imagine a man walking into a second-grade classroom and saying, "We've been having some trouble with the Hubble telescope lately. We'd like you kids to design and build a new space observatory, something we can launch next year. If you don't succeed with this, you will all be punished."

Ridiculous! There is no way children can understand the complexities of space engineering. They're just kids! That does not mean they're stupid. This particular class may actually be brilliant—for second-graders. But it is preposterous to expect them to do such advanced work.

Yet that is exactly the burden many people place on themselves. That is how many people think God treats them.

The biblical truth is liberating: God understands our weakness, He loves us for who we are, and He forgives our sins.

When people see God as an overcritical teacher, they imagine that God expects utter perfection from us, without allowing for our human frailty. They judge themselves by God's absolutely holy standards—and they find themselves falling far short.

But wait a second! Isn't that right? Doesn't God demand holiness? Doesn't He judge sin? Isn't it true that "all have sinned and fall short of the glory of God"? (Rom. 3:23)

Absolutely. But that's why Jesus died: to make us righteous. God knew that we had no hope of attaining His holy standards on our own, so He gave us some help. "God made Him who had no sin to be sin for us, so that in Him we might become the righteousness of God" (2 Cor. 5:21).

Yes, God hates sin. But He judged our sin by sending Jesus Christ to die. Now He offers us forgiveness.

The Apostle Paul made it clear that his only hope was to "be found in Him [Christ], not having a righteousness of my own that comes from the law, but that which is through faith in Christ—the righteousness that comes from God and is by faith" (Phil. 3:9).

This is Christian theology, pure and simple: We are forgiven in Christ. But while we mouth the words of these truths, they don't always sink into our hearts. Many Christians are walking around with the weight of sin on their soul, even though they trusted Christ to lift that burden long ago!

It's like a young man I know who borrowed money from his parents after he graduated from college. He was settling into a new job, a new area, and paying off a college loan, so his folks lent him a substantial amount of money—a few thousand dollars. After about a year, the parents saw that this young man was working hard, and still struggling to pay his bills, not to mention repaying their loan. So, out of love for him, they wrote it off. "It's a gift. You don't have to pay us back."

But the young man still felt an obligation. Even though he was just scraping by, he felt terrible about not repaying that "loan." He determined that someday, somehow, he would pay back his parents, and in the meantime he felt guilty for his inability to do so.

"It's a gift!" I want to say to that guy. "Accept it!" And that's what I want to say to Christians who worry about whether they're righteous enough for God. God has given us his righteousness. We should accept it.

Benefits
Psalm 103 is probably the most powerfully poetic chapter in the Bible. It's a hymn of praise to God for His compassion. In stark images, the psalmist reveals how deeply God loves us.

"Praise the Lord, O my soul," it begins.

"All my inmost being, praise His holy name." What does he praise the Lord *for?* For his "benefits" (v. 2).

What are the "benefits" of belonging to the Lord? Are we talking about a health plan, a nice vacation, or other desirable perks? Believe it or not, yes. All of the above.

> He forgives all your sins and heals all your diseases, [He] redeems your life from the pit and crowns you with love and compassion, [He] satisfies your desires with good things so that your youth is renewed like the eagle's (vv. 3-5).

But the psalm really hits its stride in verse 8.

> The Lord is compassionate and gracious, slow to anger, abounding in love. He will not always accuse, nor will He harbor His anger forever; He does not treat us as our sins deserve or repay us according to our iniquities. For as high as the heavens are above the earth, so great is His love for those who fear Him; as far as the east is from the west, so far has He removed our transgressions from us. As a father has compassion on his children, so the Lord has compassion on those who fear Him; for He knows how we are formed, He remembers that we are dust (vv. 8-14).

Let's unpack some of these statements.

The Lord is . . . slow to anger. Unlike the over-critical teacher who's always looking for a chance to yell at you, God puts up with a lot before He gets upset.

He will not always accuse, nor will He harbor His anger forever. He doesn't hold grudges. If you did something terrible as a teenager that has nagged you all your life, get rid of it. Ask God to forgive you, and it's gone.

He does not treat us as our sins deserve. Once while traveling in an unfamiliar area, I was stopped for driving 40 miles per hour in a 25 mph zone. I knew I was guilty, I just hadn't paid attention to the speed limit. But the policeman brought my license back without a ticket. "Have a nice day," he said. "And drive *carefully.*" It took me a moment to realize that I was getting off scot-free. The traffic cop was not "treating me as my sins deserved." He cut me a break. And that's what God does.

As far as the east is from the west . . . How far is that? East and west are two diametrically opposed positions. They are logical opposites. That is how far God takes our sin away from us! Many of us ask forgiveness for our sins, but we keep them in some corner of our mind. They are on the shelf somewhere to remind us how bad we really are. But God removes those sins; He sends them off to another galaxy.

As a father has compassion on his children . . .
Imagine the toddler who spreads his finger-paints all over the living room wall. He looks up at you and says, "I'm sorry." Sure, there are some parents who would send that kid to his room for a decade, but the compassionate parent has pity, and gently (though clearly) explains the problem. So God understands that we are just children.

He knows how we are formed, He remembers that we are dust. God made Adam from the dust of the earth and breathed life into him. When we try to do something apart from God's life-giving Spirit, we are just dust. God may not like this, but He understands our tendency to do so.

God Understands

A teacher I know was complaining about a troublesome student. But then she said, "His behavior really upset me until I learned about his home life. His parents divorced when he was five, and he's been bounced back and forth between them. Nobody wants him. His older brother ran away from home at sixteen, and no one went looking for him. This kid is probably abused by his stepfather, and his mother couldn't care less. It's a sad story."

What changed this teacher's attitude toward the student? His behavior was the same—just as disruptive, just as maddening—but she suddenly *understood what he was made of.* She knew where he was coming from. And so her anger turned to pity for this unloved student.

Of course the boy is still responsible for his actions. My teacher friend will still hold him accountable for his behavior, but her expectations have changed. She understands that, given his background, he may find it harder to deal with other people. He may be slow in learning appropriate social skills. Understanding that, she may cut him some slack.

But we could say that all of us come from a "broken home"—Eden. Humanity was broken by sin and continues to be plagued by sinful desires. As Christians, we wrestle with our dual nature—the Spirit urges us to do right, but deep down we are still dust.

I spoke with a woman who had been a Christian for only a year or two. She was troubled. "Why do I still have these desires to do sinful things? What's wrong with me?" I assured her that she was perfectly normal, that Christians still face temptation, and sometimes we succumb to it. I pointed her toward Romans 7 and 8, in which Paul described his own struggle with his sinful nature, and the glory of letting the Spirit take charge.

God understands our struggle. He knows what we are made of. He knows that our broken humanity often makes it difficult for us to do the right thing. He knows, because *He has been there.* Jesus became one of us, so He knows firsthand "what we are made of."

God Has Compassion on Us

We live in a world of second-guessers, back-seat drivers, and Monday morning quarter-backs. It seems that everyone is quick to tell you what you should have done, instead of what you did—especially if the choices you made had less than perfect results.

What do we tell all those after-the-fact experts? "That's easy for you to say!" Why is it "easy" to second-guess? Because they weren't there. They didn't have all the options, all the information, all the pressure that you had. They weren't walking in your shoes. If they truly put themselves in your position, under-standing all the factors that led to your deci-sions, they wouldn't be so quick to judge.

When we view God as an overcritical teacher, we assume that He's like all those other second-guessers—but He's not. God not only understands our situation, He identifies with it. He puts Himself not only in our shoes, but in our *guts*.

The Gospels depict a scene where Jesus is healing people. "When He saw the crowds, He had compassion on them, because they were harassed and helpless, like sheep with-out a shepherd" (Matt. 9:36). This was no cold, calculating Messiah-on-a-mission. He truly felt for the people who came to Him. He bore their griefs and carried their sorrows.

The English word *compassion* means to ex-perience feelings along with someone. But the

Greek word used in Matthew 9 (*splanknon*) and the Hebrew word used in Psalm 103 (*rehem*) are much stronger. Both are based on words for internal organs of the human body. The idea, quite literally, is to "feel in your gut" for someone. We come close when we say, "His heart went out to them."

This is the secret of love: to identify with other people, to put yourself in their shoes, to do unto them as you would want them to do unto you, to love your neighbor as yourself. And this is how God loves us, with a gut-level love that understands our limitations and feels our frustrations.

The Book of Hebrews talks about Jesus as our High Priest, giving us access to the Father. "For we do not have a high priest who is unable to sympathize with our weaknesses, but we have one who has been tempted in every way, just as we are—yet was without sin" (Heb. 4:15). We read of Jesus' temptation in the desert, and of His anguished prayer at Gethsemane. We don't know what other temptations He faced, but there must have been many others.

Because of these temptations, the Bible says, He understands our spiritual struggles, and *sympathizes* ("has the same feelings"). He doesn't stand there with a glowering look, saying, "Shame on you." He says, "Yeah, I know it's tough. Hang in there. Let Me help."

It doesn't mean that it's all right to sin. I'm

not saying that it doesn't matter whether we choose to do right or wrong. Sin has its own disastrous consequences. The way of dust is dry and deadly. If we get used to ignoring the call of the Spirit, we miss out on the joys of living in an intimate union with God.

But we see God in the image of the prodigal son's father, going out day by day to look for his estranged boy. The son had squandered his living and was returning home in shame and fear, after making a pack of sinful and selfish choices. "But while he was still a long way off, his father saw him and was filled with compassion for him; he ran to his son, threw his arms around him and kissed him" (Luke 15:20). The compassionate dad threw a party in the boy's honor.

But if you are in the struggle, trying to heed the Spirit, yet grappling with other desires — shamed by past struggles and afraid to come home — God understands what you are dealing with. And He's there with you at a gut level, not second-guessing, but ever-compassionate, hurting where you hurt.

God Forgives

In the wee hours of night, the phone rang. I answered sleepily, and heard a firm and formal voice say, "Dr. New, could you come to the hospital? The Wilson family would like to see you. They are in the ICU waiting room."

Mr. Wilson had been taken into the hospital

the day before, seriously stricken with a heart condition. I assumed that he was near death.

Arriving at the hospital about 2:30 A.M., I found the family discussing funeral arrangements. The doctor had said that Mr. Wilson had only another hour or so to live.

I went to his bedside and took his hand. "Warren," I said, "this is Dr. New. I've come to pray with you."

There was a very feeble squeezing of my hand. Tears flowed from his half-opened eyes. His lips moved as if to say something. I leaned close.

"Please pray," he started. His voice was halting and barely audible. "Please pray ... pray God will forgive me. I've been a hateful, bitter man all my life. I don't want to die full of hatred. I am so afraid to face God."

My heart grieved for him. He continued with great effort. "I've said mean things about you and the church ... please forgive me. Pray God will forgive me."

Through my own tears, I assured him of my forgiveness and my friendship. I also assured him of God's love. God would accept his repentant spirit.

We prayed. As I slowly voiced his desire in prayer, a beautiful experience occurred, defying the medical prognosis. I felt the strength come into his grip, literally. His eyes opened more fully, he blinked away the tears, and he said quietly but firmly, "Thank God."

Bitterness and anger and fear flowed out of him and the healing love and forgiveness of God flow in. Wholeness came that night to the soul. But healing also came to his body and, to everyone's amazement, he did not die. For several years he actively served God in his local church. He had discovered and accepted God's therapy. It began with forgiveness.

Over the years, a number of people have told me, "God could never forgive me for what I've done." I spoke with a woman who had an abortion and was wracked with guilt. There are others who have cheated on their spouses, or engaged in other sexual sins. Some are trapped in addictions to drugs or alcohol. Some are still hurting from offenses committed long ago, even in their childhood.

These often seem double-minded. One moment they try to excuse themselves, the next they're berating themselves. They quote all sorts of extenuating circumstances—"No one really understands what I was going through." But they don't convince even themselves of their own innocence. They have done wrong, and they know it. Yet they feel that God can't possibly forgive them.

Ironically, some of these people are Christians. They know all the right answers. They believe that Jesus Christ died for them, that His blood atoned for the sins of humanity. But somehow they feel that doesn't apply to them. They read that Jesus hung out with corrupt tax collectors and women of the street. Jesus forgave and welcomed and challenged these outcasts to start new lives. But today my friends fear that Jesus would judge them harshly.

How plainly can I put it?

God *understands*. He knows the extenuating circumstances. He knows your limits, your weaknesses, the pressures on you. He even knows that some of your sins weren't entirely your fault.

God *cares* deeply about you. He feels your pain. Like the prodigal's father, He wants to welcome you into a full relationship with Him.

God *forgives*. He knows that you have done wrong. No excuses, now. He knows your sins in gruesome detail. And still He loves you. By Christ's atoning death, your sins have been carted off, as far as the east is from the west. Can you let go of them too?

Questions for Reflection and Discussion

Chapters 1–2

1. Before you read these chapters, what words would you use to describe God (i.e., vindictive, compassionate)?

2. How can fear be a motivator? What about fear of God?

3. Is the "fear of the Lord" immature? Reviewing these chapters, what does Scripture have to say about that?

4. First Corinthians 13:11 speaks of "putting away childish things." Are there childish beliefs about God that you have grown beyond? How have your childhood conceptions of God changed?

5. First John 4:18 says, "Perfect love drives out fear." What does that mean?

6. Have you ever had an outstanding loan or debt canceled? How did you respond? How is this like the forgiveness of Christ?

7. In what ways do you sense God's forgiveness?

8. Psalm 103:2 refers to "benefits" God provides. What benefits are named in Psalm 103? Which apply in your own experience? What is said about God's compassion, love, and forgiveness?

9. In what ways are Christians tempted? How should we deal with temptation? (See Rom. 7–8.)

10. What does it mean to empathize? How does God empathize with His children?

Chapter Three

SO FAR AWAY

God as Absentee Father

Jason was barely seventeen and had just been arrested for the third time—drunk driving, disturbing the peace, and now petty theft. Why would this young man steal? From a well-to-do family, Jason could have anything he wanted. Well, almost anything.

The court released him to his parents, and required them to get family counseling. So they now sat in my office: the father containing his rage; the mother looking embarrassed; and Jason staring blankly out the window.

The McDowells were among the best-known families in our community, also one of the wealthiest. Jason's father owned three businesses, all very successful. These companies kept him on the road, often out of the country. He didn't have much time left for his family.

I wondered what business appointments he

was missing by being here, in counseling. He certainly gave the impression that he wished he were somewhere else.

"We have never needed counseling," Mr. McDowell huffed, "and it is quite demeaning to have to sit here and talk about problems that never should have arisen." He threw a dart of a look at his son, who wasn't paying any attention.

But, as required by the judge, the parents poured out their sad story to me. They had offered Jason everything money could buy. They had set good examples by joining several social organizations and the local country club. They had even joined a church, which they couldn't always attend because of Mr. McDowell's travel schedule. Still, they were "good Christian people, actively involved in the community."

Jason, on the other hand, was a major disappointment to them. His appearance was one thing: unkempt, dirty, ragged. It seemed that he was trying to look like a street person. But his attitude was even worse. He was flunking school and defying his teachers. He was in serious danger of not graduating. In addition, his parents knew he had been drinking since seventh grade. More than once, they had returned from social outings to find evidence of booze parties in their home. Now they suspected Jason was taking drugs too.

Ungrateful, belligerent, rebellious, Jason

didn't care about the trouble he was causing his parents. They were at their wits' end.

"He's ruining our family," the mother whined. "What will our friends think if any of this gets in the paper?"

The father added, "I've always given the boy everything. He has his own car, new clothes. We've got a nice home and he has his own room, with a stereo, TV, and computer." As he spoke, the anger simmered within him. Finally it boiled over. Turning to Jason, he yelled, "Good grief, Jason! You have it all! What more could I give you?"

Jason's answer was swift and sharp. His body shook as he pointed at his dad and said bitterly, "A little of your time!"

Those five words spoke volumes.

Jason turned back to the window and stared silently as I talked further with his parents. In the remaining minutes of that first session, I tried to give some encouragement to each member of the family. I also arranged for separate follow-up visits.

The parents missed their next appointment. My secretary got the message that Mr. McDowell was "too busy and was leaving for Europe on a trip." They never called again.

But Jason did come once, after school. I got to hear his side.

The boy had been raised by a succession of housekeepers, baby-sitters, and nannies. Summers, he was given the "privilege" of going to one elite camp after another. And in spite of having all the toys he could ever want, Jason felt alone, even abandoned.

"Why should I care?" he said. "My Dad don't!" Jason's head was bowed as he continued: "He's never around. He never has been! He never went to any of my games. He's never seen me do anything. And Mom . . . she just lives at the Racquet Club. She's hollerin' at me all the time for messin' up their lives." He mumbled something incoherent and looked slowly away, saying, "They don't really care about me. They never did."

With no positive attention from his parents, Jason settled for negative attention. Dad wouldn't come to a ball game, but he'd have to come to a hearing. Mom wouldn't give him a second glance, unless he was wearing his ripped jeans and stained T-shirt. His hardened exterior, his rebellious behavior, his obnoxious ways were all attempts to cope with and cover up his insecurity and fear—and to cry out for attention to the ones who should have been comforting him all along.

I asked Jason if he was religious at all. As a young boy, he said, he had gone to Vacation Bible School at the church his parents belonged to. For Mom and Dad it was two weeks of free baby-sitting. For Jason, it was kind of fun—except for all that talk about God.

"I just think some of those stories—you know, the Bible—I think they're a little hard to believe. As fairy tales, they're OK, I guess. But I never believed much in God. I mean, even if there is a God, He don't care about me. Like, why should He?"

Jason's attitude toward God was not unlike his attitude toward his father. Both seemed distant and uncaring—absentee fathers, at best. Jason was afraid of both, but masked his anxiety with antisocial behavior. He desperately needed to be loved and cared for, but he had learned to deny those feelings.

There are many in today's world who are like Jason. They see God as uncaring, remote, and distant. They see themselves as too small, too insignificant, or too unlovable to merit God's love or concern. Their "fear of God" is a fear of getting lost in the shuffle. They are afraid to reach out to God—that might bring rejection, judgment, pain, or they might just be ignored.

Toward the end of our session, I encouraged Jason to make contact with God. He could trust God to make things better, to make *him* better, to love him and care for him. All he needed to do was pray.

"Yeah, what if I did pray?" Jason responded. "What if I did trust God as you said and then nothing happened, nothing changed? What then? Is it worth it? I don't think so! You know, man, I just don't believe He's there!"

With those words, Jason walked away.

Lost in the Dark

Thirty-some years ago, my wife and I drove south for our honeymoon. One of our stops was the Mammoth Cave in south central Kentucky. The National Park Service guide led us along a trail deep into the ground. Gradually we left the light of day; the cave entrance disappeared behind us as a shrinking circle of brightness. Soon our path was lit only artificially, by light bulbs strung along the wall.

At one point our guide asked us to stand still, in complete silence. Throwing a tiny switch, he plunged us into total darkness.

I have never been in a place so devoid of light. Even a moonless night has a few stars or scattered beams from a house or highway. This was utter darkness. I held my wife tighter as the guide spoke.

"Think," he said, "of the first explorer of this cave, probably a Native American, edging slowly into this darkness. No railings, no proven path, only a crude torch. What if he dropped the torch, or it went out? Imagine what it would be like to be completely alone, lost in the dark, without the resources to find your way out."

It was a shuddering and fearful thought.

Some people feel as if they live their whole life in a cave like that. The light of God has long ago disappeared behind them. They feel trapped in utter darkness. They may hear noises from above, and know that others are

dancing in the daylight, but they are sure that
no one up there knows or cares about them,
down there, in the pit.

The Light Fades

I counseled a young woman named Amy who
had decided, in the painful aftermath of a romantic breakup, that God just didn't care
about her. She had grown up in the Baptist
church, raised her hand in Vacation Bible
School, learned the memory verses. But now
she was hurting, badly. This time, she figured,
God had not come through.

Amy had always had a tender soul. She felt
guilty at the drop of a Sunday School pin. She
strove to be a model believer, so that God
would not be disappointed in her. She feared
what would ever happen if she went astray.
As a child, she was the type of person we
discussed in chapter 1, fearing God as an
"overcritical teacher." She was fanatical about
doing the right thing.

In a way, that's what got her into trouble.

In junior high, she invited a friend to come
to her church. The friend agreed, if Amy
would return the favor by visiting her Episcopal church. Amy agreed. So the friend visited
the Baptist church, but when Amy explained
to her youth leader that she'd be going the
next Sunday (to visit the Episcopal church),
she was forbidden to do so. She tried to explain the arrangement, to no avail.

Amy was torn. She had been taught to keep her promises. She had been taught to bring visitors to church. But now the church was keeping her from keeping her promise. As it turned out, she obeyed the youth leader and broke the promise to her friend—but she began to question many things at her church.

At the same time, Amy's father was growing more distant. They had laughed and played together when she was a little girl, but now in her teenage years, he merely barked and growled and read the paper. She was mystified by it, worrying that she must have done something wrong. She found herself descending into a dark cave, and she didn't know why. Her church, her father, and her God were increasingly out of reach. She didn't know what to do.

She spent her adolescence frantically trying to claw her way back into God's good graces, but she received little affirmation from anyone who mattered. In college she found romance with a young man, a Christian. Finally, here was someone who affirmed her, who appreciated her—a ray of light in her dark life. She clung to him like a lifeline.

Maybe she was clinging too tightly. The man got as far as an engagement, but then suddenly broke it off. Amy pled with him, and prayed to God. "Please, don't let this flicker of light fade!"

But he was gone. She was destroyed. All

her prayers just stuck to the ceiling—they didn't seem to go anywhere. And Amy decided God was far away and couldn't be bothered. God was reading the paper somewhere, or watching some heavenly ball game. He had no time for her. Or so she feared.

Why So Distant?

How many people are there in this world like Amy or Jason? Unquestionably more than we know. What gives them the idea that God is far away? It could be any number of things:

The example of a distant earthly father. Jason had an absentee earthly father, and Amy's dad moved away from her emotionally. Like so many people in this broken world, they transferred the same father-feelings to their Heavenly Father. Those of us who have been blessed with loving, attentive fathers often assume that the image of God as Father means the same thing to everyone—a caring God who's there when you need Him. But many people have a very different idea of what a father is. He's the guy who shows up every other weekend, if he's not too busy; he's the guy who beats me; he's the one who fights with Mom. It's natural for these people to assume that this is what "father" means. If God is our "Father, which art in heaven," then He must be just like that, only farther away. Or so people think.

A church's emphasis on God's distance. When Isaiah had his vision, he saw the Lord "high and exalted" (Isa. 6:1). The angels sang of God's holiness, and Isaiah counted himself unworthy of God's message. But that same vision shows God longing for a relationship with His people, and making Isaiah worthy to bear the message. Many churches today focus on God's distant holiness and forget the relationship He wants with us. They urge parishioners to live lives worthy of God's holiness, but they sometimes leave out the idea that God's Spirit is within us, helping us to achieve that.

Imagined guilt for unspecified sins. When you have a tender soul like Amy's, it doesn't take much to make you confess to anything and everything. We talk about sins of omission and commission and secret sins and bad attitudes; and if you insist you're not guilty of any of those, surely you have the sin of pride. As a result, many people go around feeling generally guilty. For what? They're not sure, but there must be something.

These are the people who go forward at altar calls nine or ten times a year, "just to make sure." I knew a woman who felt like sneaking out of the church during altar calls, just so her sinfulness would not keep God from working. I am not making fun of such people. I am suggesting that we talk too much about self-examination and not enough about forgiveness. We foster a vague sense of guilt that keeps God out of reach for many people.

Real guilt for real sin. Of course, some people *do* have sin in their lives. Perhaps they are living in sinful relationships, or holding grudges, or letting the love of money rule their lives. They like what they're doing, but they're learning that they can't serve two masters. God seems increasingly distant to them because they insist on clinging to sin.

You have probably seen the quip, "If God seems far away . . . guess who moved!" In general, I don't like this statement because, as we have seen, there are other reasons that people might feel this way. But, in the case of sin, the person *has* moved away from God. Still, forgiveness is available. All a person has to do is turn around, turn his or her back on sin, and seek the Lord.

Dashed expectations of what God would do. Many people are, in author Philip Yancey's words, "disappointed with God." They prayed for something, and it didn't happen. They lived well, and disaster still came upon them. A husband left, a car was totaled, a best friend was diagnosed with cancer. They had assumed that there was a basic justice in the world, that good people would get good things, but now it seems that just the reverse is true. How do you make sense of that? One way is to think that God must be so far away that He doesn't notice what's happening.

For whatever reason, many people feel neglected by God. They assume that, if they call on God, they'll just get a busy signal, so they don't even try to get through.

I have a friend, a science fiction buff, who had a recurring dream. She saw herself floating in space, with no connection to any spaceship, cut off from all life support. She could see Planet Earth in the distance, a bright orb spinning happily against the dark backdrop of space. She knew that life was going on there, but she was lost in space. She was afraid that she would die there, all alone, and no one would know.

This image mirrored her earthbound life. She believed in God, but He seemed far away. She saw Him at work in other people, but she considered herself unworthy of His attention. When her husband left her, she felt stranded—but she couldn't bring herself to pray for guidance. Why should God care?

Life without God's active presence is a cold, dank place, a lightless cave. My friend languished there in the dark—feeling abandoned, alone, and afraid.

She desperately need to hear the psalmist's words:

Where can I go from Your Spirit? Where can I flee from Your presence? If I go up to the heavens, You are there; if I make my bed in the depths, You are there. If I rise on the wings of the dawn, if I settle on the far side of the sea, even there Your hand will guide me, Your right hand will hold me fast. If I say, "Surely the darkness will hide me and the light become night around me," even the darkness will not be dark to You; the night will shine like the day, for darkness is as light to You (Ps. 139:7-12).

Chapter Four

PRESENT AND ACCOUNTED FOR

God Walks with Us

Picture a small child in a busy shopping mall. For a moment, he loses his grip on Mommy's hand. She's only five feet away, but all this little boy knows is that *she's not holding his hand anymore*. People are rushing by on either side. At two feet tall, it's a frightening scene — strange pant legs and coat hems and jostling packages. Where's Mommy?

The boy stands there and wails.

In a microsecond, the loving mother is kneeling beside him, drying her son's tears, taking him in her arms, whispering words of reassurance: "I'm here. I was right nearby. You're all right. I'm here now."

When we see God as an absentee Father, we can feel like that child in the mall. People rush past us, but we have no idea where we are, where we're going, or how we're going to get out of the mess we're in.

But if we only cry out to Him, He will be there for us, whispering His gentle words of comfort:

> I have chosen you and have not rejected you. So do not fear, for I am with you; do not be dismayed, for I am your God. I will strengthen you and help you; I will uphold you with My righteous right hand. . . . For I am the Lord, your God, who takes hold of your right hand and says to you, Do not fear; I will help you (Isa. 41:9-10, 13).

Again and again in the Scriptures we hear words of comfort from God to His people. Certainly, God is presented as the Almighty Creator, full of glory and majesty. Yes, He is seen as "high and exalted"—but that's not the whole story. He promises His presence. He is with us!

In the well-known 23rd Psalm, David the shepherd-king pictured God not as a distant monarch, but as a caring herdsman: "Even though I walk through the valley of the shadow of death, I will fear no evil, for *You are with me*" (v. 4, italics added).

There is no paradox here. God is the King who Cares; the Holy One who Understands. The psalmist says, "The Lord confides in those who fear Him; He makes His covenant known to them" (Ps. 25:14). We find fear and confiding in the same sentence! It doesn't seem to match. It's like strict Miss McGillicuddy sitting down with her history class and passing notes with the rest of them. But God does not set Himself up far away from us. Without losing one ounce of His holiness, He sits down next to us and draws us close, filling us in on all the great promises in store for us.

The Search Party

Despite those promises, there were times in Israel's history when God seemed far away. Enemies invaded and wreaked havoc in the land, even desecrating the holy places. God's "chosen people" were taken captive and, when they returned, their country was in shambles. It seemed that God had left town—an absentee Father if ever there was one.

"Why do You always forget us?" asked the tortured writer of Lamentations. "Why do You forsake us so long?" (Lam. 5:20) We even get some of that cave mentality—deep in a subterranean darkness:

> He has made me dwell in darkness like those long dead. He has walled me in so I cannot escape; He has weighed me down with chains. Even when I call out or cry for help, He shuts out my prayer. He has barred my way with blocks of stone (3:6-9).

Yet even this writer sounds a note of hope. All is not lost. It could be worse. Salvation may yet arrive:

Yet this I call to mind and therefore I have hope: Because of the Lord's great love we are not consumed, for His compassions never fail. They are new every morning; great is Your faithfulness. . . . The Lord is good to those whose hope is in Him, to the one who seeks Him; it is good to wait quietly for the salvation of the Lord (vv. 21-26).

In the midst of disaster, God confided His plans of future glory. At some point, He would be turning on the lights. When the Northern Kingdom of Israel was being swept away by the bloodthirsty Assyrians, the Prophet Isaiah predicted a time when "there will be no more gloom for those who were in distress. In the past He humbled the land of Zebulun and the land of Naphtali [northern tribes], but in the future He will honor Galilee [in that same northern area]. . . . The people walking in darkness have seen a great light; on those living in the land of the shadow of death a light has dawned" (Isa. 9:1-2).

He went on to talk about the coming Ruler who would accomplish this. A child would be born, who would be a Wonderful Counselor, the Mighty God, the Everlasting Father, the

Prince of Peace. Sure enough, it was in Galilee where Jesus conducted most of His ministry (Matt. 4:13-16).

Isaiah also prophesied that this child would be called "Immanuel," a Hebrew term for "God with us" (Isa. 7:14). That doesn't necessarily mean that that name would appear on the birth certificate, but it does introduce a fascinating concept about the *nature* of this child. All of God's promises — "Do not be afraid; I am with you" — would now be wrapped up in this baby, and in the man He would become. He would embody the presence of God among His people. Could it be that the promised child would be God in human flesh?

Elsewhere, the prophet said this Promised One would be specially appointed, an Anointed One ("Messiah" in Hebrew), sent "to open eyes that are blind, to free captives from prison and to release from the dungeon those who sit in darkness" (Isa. 42:7). He was the search party sent to find the people stranded in the darkness of the cave. He would shine His light and lead them out of their dungeon.

When Jesus began His public ministry, He stood up in a synagogue in Galilee and read from another chapter of Isaiah: "He has sent me to bind up the brokenhearted, to proclaim freedom for the captives and release for the prisoners" (61:1). Then He sat down and said merely, "Today this Scripture is fulfilled in your hearing" (Luke 4:18).

He was the Promised One. As the Apostle Paul put it later, "He came and preached peace to you who were far away and peace to those who were near" (Eph. 2:17). That peace, of course, was accomplished not just through Jesus' preaching, but through His sacrificial death. "You who once were far away have been brought near *through the blood of Christ,*" Paul wrote (v. 13, italics added).

Camping Out with Us

The Apostle John used a term from the Greek thinkers to describe who Jesus was. He called him *Logos.* That is usually translated as "The Word," but it's rich in philosophical meaning. *Logos* was the eternal governing principle of the universe. It was the reason that all things existed. If modern physicists ever come up with a unified theory, that's the *Logos* the Greeks were looking for. It was the ultimate heavenly ideal, of which all things on earth are just a cheap copy.

So John starts his Gospel with this *Logos,* describing how it was "in the beginning with God" and was, in fact, God Himself. And so far, you can imagine all sorts of philosophy students nodding their heads. "Oh, yeah, this is exactly what Professor Plotinus was telling us." John says *Logos* participated in the Creation, and was essential to it, bringing light and life. The students are still nodding.

But then John explains that this *Logos,* that distant eternal principle, "became flesh and made His dwelling among us" (John 1:14). The eternal principle of the universe became a human being and lived next door to humans! A few of those students just swallowed their gum.

As Eugene Peterson puts it in his paraphrase, *The Message,* "The Word became flesh and blood and moved into the neighborhood." He is with us, on our turf.

The Greek word for "made His dwelling" carries the idea of pitching a tent. I remember how impressed I was, as a boy, when one of the church leaders would accompany the youth group on a camping trip. These were people I admired from afar. I always saw them up there at the pulpit, making announcements or leading the singing. They were distant and revered. But then they put on flannel shirts and trekked with us into the wilderness. They pitched their tents with us and slept on the same cold ground. They were there with us.

And that's what kind of God we serve— One who camps out with us, One who knows every pebble on our path, One who stretches out on the same cold ground. Jesus left the glories of heaven and poured Himself out upon the earth, becoming not only human, but a poor human, a homeless human, a human who was killed as a criminal.

When we wonder how we're going to pay

the rent, He knows what we're going through; He's been there. When we suffer insult and indignity, He knows what we're going through; He's been there. When our bodies are wracked with pain or disease, He knows . . . He knows.

The fact is that God never wants to stay far away from us. Christ came for the express purpose of bringing people close to God. "We have peace with God through our Lord Jesus Christ," Paul says in the Book of Romans, "through whom we have *gained access* by faith into this grace in which we now stand. . . . we have now received *reconciliation*" (Rom. 5:1-2, 11, italics added). The door isn't shut anymore. The curtain separating God from His people has been torn in two. A way has been opened. The faraway is now near.

Pocket Counselor

Here's an idea for a computer gizmo that will revolutionize the world—the Pocket Counselor. So many people are going to professional counselors these days—psychiatrists and psychologists and what-have-you—and people pay $75, $100 per visit. Surely we can rig up a machine where you type in your problems and receive a computerized response! Sell it for $49.95, and we'll make a killing. (Just remember who gave you this idea.)

We've got to make it small enough to carry around in your pocket. Then, if you're walking down the street and you suddenly have some self-defeating thoughts, just pull out your Pocket Counselor and say, "I feel that I'm a bad person."

The Voice Recognition chip will interpret your comments and respond (on screen or, for a few dollars more, with its Voice Synthesis chip), "I hear you saying you feel that you're a bad person. There, there now. It's probably your parents' fault. Have a nice day."

We could rig it with a sensor that reads your body temperature, pulse, and so on. Whenever you become anxious about something, the machine goes into Calming Mode: "It will be all right. Don't worry. It will turn out fine. Have a nice day."

I think there's a bundle to be made here. And if the product goes well, then we can spin out the Pocket Counselor *at Law,* which will dispense legal advice at the flick of a transistor. "These would-be business partners don't seem honest, George. Get out of the deal when you can. Have a nice day."

What a concept! Your own personal adviser, offering encouragement, challenge, and advice whenever you need it!

Unfortunately, it's already been done in a much more effective manner. Jesus promised His disciples that the Father would send a "Counselor to be with you forever—the Spirit of truth" (John 14:16-17). He added: "The Counselor, the Holy Spirit, whom the Father will send in My name, will teach you all things and will remind you of everything I have said to you" (v. 26). Our little Personal Counselor is already obsolete.

The Greek word used for Counselor in these texts is *parakletos* (occasionally you may hear scholars refer to the "Paraclete"). Literally, it means *one who is called alongside*. It's a passive word with an active meaning—the Paraclete *is called* in order to *do* things. Think over the million courtroom dramas you've seen. The lawyer is hired or appointed to stand alongside a person in court and do all the work for that person. That's the role of the Paraclete. (In fact, the Greek word *parakletos* was also used for lawyers.)

A young man told me of the joy of tutoring a child in an inner-city ministry. He was helping a girl with her math homework. They were working on simple percentages. "Oh, no," she said. "I left my calculator at home."

My friend said, "You don't need a calculator. You can figure that out in your head." At first, she didn't believe it, but with his prodding, she was able to work out every problem correctly. She didn't need an electronic calculator! She was smart enough to do it herself!

That too is the role of the Paraclete—a tutor, sitting alongside, not working out your problems for you, but empowering you to work them out yourself.

The Holy Spirit lives within the hearts of

those who have trusted Christ. He is always
with us, offering assurance, encouragement,
advice, challenge, correction.

O Lord, You have searched me and You
know me," the psalmist sings. "You
know when I sit and when I rise; You
perceive my thoughts from afar. You discern my going out and my lying down;
You are familiar with all my ways. Before
a word is on my tongue You know it
completely, O Lord (Ps. 139:1-4).

The Lord knows us better than we know
ourselves. He knows what we need before we
even ask. In one of the few explicit Old Testament references to the third person of the
Trinity, the psalmist continues:

Where can I go from Your Spirit? Where
can I flee from Your presence? If I go up
to the heavens, You are there; if I make
my bed in the depths, You are there. If I
rise on the wings of the dawn, if I settle
on the far side of the sea, even there
Your hand will guide me, Your right hand
will hold me fast (vv. 7-10).

No matter how far away we may feel, the
Spirit is right there with us, providing what
we need, if we will only accept it. As one
hymn states, He is "beside us, to guide us."

He is the light on the miner's helmet, leading safely through dark caves.

Bible scholar William Barclay called the Spirit "the person who nerves the feeble for the battle and who makes the coward brave, the person who gives us wise counsel and powerful help in the difficult decisions of life, the person who is for us the prisoner's friend when we face the judgment of God."

So God has not set Himself far away from us. He has walked among us in the person of Jesus Christ, and He lives within the hearts of believers through His Holy Spirit.

Yes, You!

If you feel that God is far away, however, all this theology may not do you much good. As I've talked with people in that frame of mind, I've been amazed at their persistence in believing that the promises of Scripture *do not apply to them*. They are somewhat like the writer of Psalm 73, who stated: "Surely God is good to Israel . . . but *as for me,* my feet had almost slipped" (Ps. 73:1, italics added).

In this way of thinking, people can agree that God is good . . . to everyone else. They feel that somehow they missed the last train to the Promised Land. They wander in the dark cave, hearing the voices of happy, smiling people in the distance, but they feel lost.

One woman told me about such a time in her life, before she became a Christian. She was visiting a church and heard a vocalist sing a song entitled, "Lord, Let Me Be Like You." It was a simple ditty, asking God to empower the singer to live righteously—but this woman came away thinking, "How conceited can you get, to think that you could ever be like God!" To expect the high and holy God to share His nature with you, well, as she saw it, that was the height of hubris. She could never be on such familiar terms with God. Maybe others could sing songs like that, but this woman was sure that she never would.

She was wrong.

A few months later, in a time of great emotional need, she called on God to help her, and He did. She dared to think that God's promises actually applied to her. With the help of loving friends and a great church, she came to see that Jesus died *for her,* not just for everyone else. She took the hand of the Lord who had been close to her all along.

As Paul told the Athenians, God wants people to "seek Him and perhaps reach out for Him and find Him, though *He is not far from each one of us*" (Acts 17:27). If you fear that God is far away, take a chance on reaching out to Him. You'll see just how close He is.

Running Away

But there are also Christians who feel far away from God, and who know the fear that distance brings. There are several reasons people might feel this way, and one of them is simple — sin.

Sin is a separator; it builds walls. When we do what God doesn't like, we are turning away from God. God may seem far away from us because we have moved away from Him.

The solution, however, is simple. Say you're sorry. Confess your sin to God, and He will forgive you through the blood of Christ. He stands ready to welcome you back, if you will only turn back to Him.

Yet we often make it more difficult than it has to be. Some Christians suffer from *an overwhelming sense of guilt*. They are sure that *their* sin is unforgivable, or that God must be tired of forgiving them, or that surely they have proven how rotten they are. They may be sorry, and they may even confess their sins, but they don't accept God's forgiveness! They don't turn around and step into God's waiting embrace. They fear that they are too guilty for God.

Let me repeat the clear message of Scripture. God longs to forgive us. That's why Jesus died, so that God could pay for our sin. *We don't have to.* We just have to accept the free gift of this relationship with God. The same grace that bought our eternal salvation continues to bring us back into fellowship with God, even after we have hurt Him with our sin. "The Lord is compassionate and gracious, slow to anger, abounding in love" (Ps.

103:8). Accept His forgiveness and come home.

Other people just *don't want to give up their sin*. They cling so tightly to their illicit pleasures that they cannot turn back to God. "If I get right with God, do I have to stop this affair I'm having?" Well, yes. God forgives your sin, but in order for you to live in a close relationship with the Lord, you need to ditch the sin that's separating you.

Yet some are so blinded by the temporary pleasures of sin, that they ignore the greater value of the wholeness God offers. They are like the rich young man who came to Jesus, was challenged to forsake his greedy ways, and went away sadly, because he had too many things. People like this keep their distance from God because they want to serve two masters, and they just can't.

Trying Times

And then there are people like Job, who see everything going wrong and wonder why. God seems strangely distant and life is tough and what is going on anyway?

All your neighbors, like Job's friends, are quick to say, "There must be sin in your life." But you have scoured your soul and you know better. With Job, you say to God, "Do not condemn me, but tell me what charges You have against me" (Job 10:2). Yet He remains silent. Does He care anymore?

"If only there were someone to arbitrate between us," Job agonized, ". . . someone to remove God's rod from me, so that His terror would frighten me no more" (Job 9:33-34). Such times are fearsome indeed.

When a child learns to ride a bike, at first Mom or Dad is probably walking (or running) alongside, holding the bike, making sure it doesn't fall. But if the parent stays there, year after year, there's something wrong. "Hey, Dad, it's time for my paper route. You need to run along and hold the bike!" That's not the way it's supposed to work.

In the same way, God allows us to face trials so that we might grow spiritually. It may seem that God is far away, but He is not. He never lets us out of His sight. Like the mother who follows her child around the block on his "trial run" with the bicycle, God is close behind us, making sure we'll be OK.

"Consider it pure joy, my brothers, whenever you face trials of many kinds," writes James, "because you know that the testing of your faith develops perseverance. Perseverance must finish its work so that you may be mature and complete, not lacking anything" (James 1:2-4).

God is not absent. Sometimes for our own good He steps back into the shadows, but He is always ready to help us, whether we recognize that or not.

Questions for Reflection and Discussion

Chapters 3–4

1. In what situations has God seemed distant or uncaring to you? Why did you perceive Him that way?

2. How would you define guilt? In what ways are Christians sometimes caught in false or unmerited guilt?

3. How can we discern between false guilt and true guilt? How do we come to know what God really expects of us?

4. Review Psalm 139:7-12. What do these words say about God's proximity?

5. At what times or in what ways has God come close to you?

6. Reflect on the image of "God camping out with us" (John 1:14). What difference does that make in your understanding of Him?

7. Jesus promised that the Counselor, the Holy Spirit, would come to us (John 14). How does the Spirit work in your life?

8. What attitudes, thoughts, or actions might keep a person from sensing God's closeness?

Chapter Five

GETTING
THE JOB DONE

God as a No-Nonsense Boss

The man was a great Christian leader. Active in inner-city ministry, he had even founded an orphanage. He might have had a great career in business, but he gave his organizational abilities to the work of the Lord, sacrificing earthly success for heavenly treasure. Everyone spoke highly of him.

He had three children who admired him greatly, though he wasn't home as much as they'd like. He was always at work, or at meetings, or traveling the country to raise support. He was a loving father when he was home, however, and his kids loved his company. But they learned quickly that they had to share him with others.

Once, this father planned to take his children to a major league baseball game. It was a big deal, and the kids dreamed about it for weeks in advance. Finally, for one glorious night, their dad would be all theirs. But at the last minute, the father decided to get some extra tickets and bring some kids from the orphanage along. His own children were left feeling like orphans themselves.

Put yourself in their shoes. What can you say? Can you call your dad a bad guy for taking orphans to a ball game? No! He's doing the work of the Lord. But meanwhile your need to be special, your natural desire for a father who will spend time with you, goes unmet. Yet you feel guilty and greedy for wanting a father when those orphans have none. God is obviously on Dad's side of this issue, or so it seems.

In a situation like this, you learn that the whole Bible can be summed up in one commandment: "Just get the job done!" There are always people out there who need the Gospel, who need a helping hand. How dare you enjoy the luxury of fun, of family, of love, when all those lonely voices are crying in the city! Who do you think you are?

I need to tread carefully here. We *do* have work to do as Christians. Evangelism and helping ministries are important pursuits for believers, but when the pressure to "get the job done" squeezes all joy and love out of the Christian life, something is wrong. Yet thousands of people see God as a taskmaster, a demanding foreman, a workaholic father.

They fear that He will be displeased unless they are constantly working for His kingdom.

In describing this view, I'm not just comparing God to the father who's never home. It's the father who considers his work the most important thing in his life. Not only is he often at the job, but his mind seems to be always *in* the job. Even at home, he's noodling some problem he faced that day. He doesn't know how to relax, to kick back, to have fun. He's a no-nonsense dad, running his home like an office or factory, running his life by his Daytimer.

You've known people like this, haven't you? Even their occasional moments of fun are strictly regimented. "Birthday party, eight to eight-thirty; then conference call with Grandma and Grandpa." Vacations are more tiring than real life—"We only have five hours for Disneyland, so let's fan out. George, you take the rides. Molly, you can do 'Small World,' only don't start singing that silly song all the time. Chrissy, you meet the cartoon characters. But everyone's back here at 3. Gotta make the Grand Canyon by noon tomorrow."

That seems ridiculous, of course. But that's not far from the image of God that many Christians have. The work is all-important. No time to relax.

Again, I'm not saying that our work as Christians is *un*important. But it needs to be seen in the context of a *relationship* with God that is loving and joyful. We work because we love Him, He loves us, and we want to extend His love to others. If we work because we're afraid that, on Judgment Day, He'll turn to us and say, "Couldn't you have done a little bit more?"—we're missing the point.

The Work of Evangelism

I have great respect for those who invest their lives in the work of telling others about Jesus. I've known hundreds of missionaries and evangelistic preachers, and I've known other lay people with a gift for leading others to Christ. Many of these work tirelessly to welcome people into God's kingdom.

But the best evangelists I know have been those who knew how to laugh. They're the ones who truly *like* people. They share God's burden of compassion for those who don't know Him yet, but they also share God's joy in relating to people.

Believe it or not, I've met some evangelists who didn't seem to like people. It's not up to me to judge what's in their hearts, but they gave every indication that they really didn't enjoy the people they talked with. If your focus is on getting *decisions* for Christ, you can begin to see people as *obstacles* to those decisions. "I've explained it as clearly as I can! Why don't they accept it?"

Some evangelists, especially those who travel from city to city, can get into the *num-*

bers trap. "We got eighteen conversions last week and only twelve this week. What am I doing wrong?" Suddenly salvation is a commodity. Eighteen of this, twelve of that—you might as well be selling stock futures. What happened to the "rejoicing in heaven over one sinner who repents"? (Luke 15:7) When your focus is on the work, you can lose sight of the relationships.

Churches that concentrate on outreach and training are susceptible to the *assembly-line mentality.* I have heard the process described something like this: "We get a new believer in our church, and we put her into the soul-winning course. In six weeks, she wins someone else to the Lord. Then we put *that* person in our soul-winning course, and that person brings in someone else, and so on."

It's great that people are coming to know the Lord, but are they really "coming to *know* the Lord"? When do they have time to truly get to know Jesus, when they're slapped into a course and sent out to win someone else? Programs like this make me wonder, "What are these people being converted *to*?" Do we just get them to agree to a particular theology, or are we welcoming them into a relationship with God?

Again, let me say that I'm not opposed to evangelism training courses. But I would warn the trainees to guard against a mentality that sees people just as cogs in a machine.

They are *people,* with whom God wants a friendship. We have the privilege of extending to them an invitation to God's party.

I would also urge churches to develop well-rounded ministries, which involve worship celebrations, caring fellowship, and support times, as well as evangelism training. We need to experience the relationship with God that we're inviting others into.

The Work of Helping Those in Need

I talked with a young missionary who had come home early from the African nation where she was serving. She was shell-shocked. The need in that place was overwhelming. She saw hunger and abject poverty, violence and oppression. She longed to help, but there was so little she could do.

In such cases, a person asks, "What good am I? I can feed one little boy today, but he'll starve next week. Am I doing any good?"

My missionary friend came home early because, frankly, she was going a little crazy. Since childhood, she had set her sights on foreign missions. But once she got to the field, she was blindsided by the terrible conditions. It wasn't that she craved luxury for herself—she was more than willing to suffer with the people she served. But would that do any good? She was eager to "get the job done," but that seemed impossible because "the job" was so huge.

Those who see God as a no-nonsense task-master push themselves emotionally and physically. "How can I eat when they go hungry? How can I relax when they must work day and night? How can I enjoy myself when they are always on the brink of death?" They are afraid that God will be disappointed if they don't "go the distance." But where is that "distance"? Does it make any sense to become a casualty yourself?

These are tough questions.

Let's bring it closer to home. I've known a number of inner-city workers in similar straits. They too are serving in areas of great need. They see hunger, poverty, oppression, and violence. They work day and night to save as many as they can from their cruel society. These people seem tired, embattled, over-worked. Often they burn out.

And I've known too many pastors who suffered from ministry burnout. They took the weight of their whole congregation on their shoulders and didn't know when to say stop. People came night and day with their needs, and these ministers could not turn them down. They were afraid to say no, afraid that God would be disappointed in them.

One key Scripture comes to mind. When a woman poured some expensive perfume on Jesus' feet in an act of worship, the disciples remarked that the perfume could have been sold and the money given to feed the poor.

Jesus made the surprising comment, "The poor you will always have with you" (Matt. 26:11).

It's surprising because Jesus, more than anyone before or since, displayed a compassion for the poor. This comment seems calloused, cynical, coming from our loving Lord. But it's important to consider what He meant.

He was *not* saying that ministry to the poor is worthless. He was not saying that we should ignore the poor because they'll always be poor anyway. That would go against everything else He said and did. He *was* saying that we need to worship too. Only when we kneel in worship at Jesus' feet does our service to the poor really mean anything. Helping the poor is an important ministry, but it is not the be-all and end-all of Christianity. Our Christian service needs to flow from our relationship with Christ. And that joyful relationship continually nourishes and restores us.

The Work of Personal Holiness

Noted journalist H.L. Mencken once described Puritanism as "the haunting fear that someone, somewhere, may be happy." That's actually historically inaccurate—the Puritans who settled New England were really rather fun-loving, but the same description might apply to a number of modern-day Christians.

Such people are so intent on being "separate from the world" that they miss out on the God-given joy of life. They assume that any human pleasure is an affront to God's holiness, or at least a distraction from the pursuit of holiness. Once there were monks who whipped themselves on the back in order to suffer with Christ. Nowadays people just refuse to have fun.

People like this may spend an hour each day in prayer and Bible study, but they feel guilty that they don't spend two. There is always more to do; they are never satisfied. True spirituality, they feel, means rooting out every ounce of "self" within you—and so they put themselves down for all sorts of normal behavior. "If I were really a good Christian, I'd let that person ahead of me in the grocery-store line."

I affirm the desire to please Christ. And I admire the discipline that many of these people have. But I think they're missing some major ingredients of Christian faith—laughter, peace, creative praise, outrageous joy.

This was more of a problem, I think, thirty or forty years ago. In general, Christians have lightened up. There are both good and bad aspects of this change. It's true that many Christians are rather casual about personal holiness today.

But, even when people are having fun in their daily lives, they often divide that from their spiritual lives. In many cases, they still treat everything religious with a somber attitude. "Let's stop having fun now; it's time to be spiritual." The church doors open and the joy is turned off. Many of us learned that pattern as children—one mustn't run around and play in God's house—and I'm sure there was some value in teaching respect for the Lord. But too many have never grown out of that. They are still refusing to "play" in God's house. God presents His truth to us in parables and poems, riddles and rhymes, but too many of us aren't getting into the game.

The Great Escape

Nancy sat near the front of the college science class I taught. She was attentive, always on time with her lessons, and well above average in her test scores. The one thing she did not do—and would not do—was to participate in class discussion. Though half the semester had passed, I had never heard her speak. Her major class project was due in only two weeks, and that required an oral report.

With only days left, she stopped at my office door. Without looking up, she softly asked to speak with me. I stood, invited her in, and offered a chair. She was shy and frightened.

"How may I help you?" I asked.

She continued to look at the floor, and spoke slowly and softly. "Mr. New," she said, "I like your science class, but I am sorry I can't do my oral report. I just can't do it. I hope ..." She trailed off and I picked up the conversation.

"You can't do your report?" I questioned.

"No, sir, I just can't. I've been dreading it all semester. I can't talk in front of people. I never have!"

I sensed her anxiety was far deeper than the normal stage fright suffered by most students.

"Haven't you ever given a speech?" I asked her. "What about high school?"

"No sir, I've never . . ." She paused, then added, "Well, I never had to. I always avoided being in front of the class. I've always been afraid to do anything, period!" She looked up with a fleeting glance, obviously very nervous about sitting before me.

There was some other issue here. It wasn't just a matter of going solo before her peers. She seemed fearful about everything. I wanted to know more.

"Where are you from, Nancy? How long have you been on campus?"

Her story was pathetic. Nancy had come to our campus from an Eastern state. The oldest of several children, she was using college more for escape than for education. Though Nancy was in her second year at the school, I didn't remember seeing her on our small campus before she came to my class. When I mentioned this, she laughed nervously.

"Oh, no, Mr. New, I don't do much but go to class. I want to do more, but I'm just afraid." Again, she grew very quiet.

"It's OK, Nancy, but tell me what are you so fearful of?"

"Everything," she replied. "I've always been afraid, and I hate it."

"You've always been afraid?" I repeated.

"Yes, always. In high school . . . even in grade school, I was always afraid to do anything. I wanted so badly to have fun and laugh and make friends and go to the school things . . . but my dad wouldn't let me."

"Oh, your dad . . ." I began, but she cut me off.

"He wouldn't even let us laugh!" she said sharply. "Mr. New, I can't do anything without feeling like a sinner. I don't go to any school functions, I don't have any real friends, I've never even had a date. . . . Mr. New, I don't even eat in the cafeteria. I just get my food and take it to my room."

I was now very sure a classroom report was only a superficial matter. Nancy's anxieties were long-term and broad in effect.

That was the beginning of a year-and-a-half of counseling. Nancy's father was an ultra-fundamental and pharisaical keeper of a strict religious code of conduct. His idea of Christianity and Jesus bordered on the morbid. Children were to be seen, not heard. They were to be subservient at all times. They were not to play with children outside their home. They were forbidden to laugh. Laughter and play were of the devil, inappropriate for Christians. Nancy had been dressed plainly by her parents and had been forced to wear boys' high-top work shoes until she was fourteen. She had been forbidden to date, have boys as friends, go to parties, or do anything that even looked fun. At the same time, she had never been taught even the basic things about her own body, about human reproduction, or sexuality. What she had learned, she had gotten from books, but felt "dirty" and guilty. Her father had forced his family to go to church, to pray regularly, and to sit for hours in quiet times meditating. Any frivolity was strictly forbidden.

Nancy had grown up believing that God was an absolute no-nonsense, no-fun, no-laughter God. Very early she had learned to avoid people and informal situations where she felt any joy. She grew more and more reclusive, yet she longed to escape. This feeling, coupled with a growing resentment of her parents and the home, led her to leave for this Christian college. It also left her with a neurotic fear of God and a sense that she was constantly displeasing Him. Her curiosity about boys, her desire to go to parties, her natural need to have fun—these were all sources of guilt and discomfort.

Only after months of counseling, reading assignments, and gradual experiments with socialization did Nancy begin to feel "normal." She eventually began to date, to attend school functions, and to laugh freely. Her understanding of God and His love also matured. By her senior year, she had become active in a variety of school and church activities. She was also elected May Queen, and after graduation became a public school teacher. A few years later, I had the privilege of performing Nancy's wedding.

An abnormal fear of God usually results from a sense of guilt, whether real or false. Guilt, of course, is based on your perceptions of right and wrong. Nancy grew up in a joyless system which imposed guilt for all sorts of innocent acts. This greatly inhibited her personal and spiritual development. She was caught between her strong desire to escape from this oppressive regime and the strong guilt-system which had been instilled in her.

With time and great effort, Nancy worked through her guilt to find a new and healthy understanding of God. It helped her to know that I had accepted her and did not think badly of her, though she had told me all the things she had done and thought were wrong. She came to realize that God accepted her even when she felt guilty. With this new sense of acceptance, she began growing in a friendly relationship with God. She learned a system of forgiveness and joy from her loving Heavenly Father quite unlike the system of guilt she had learned from her earthly father.

Chapter Six

THE LORD OF LAUGHTER

God Loves Parties

I was having breakfast with my good friend
Steve Bell. We had both been on the road in
recent weeks, so this was a nice time to catch
up with each other, to share stories, to laugh
together and relax. We ordered our food and,
as we waited, Steve told me a very funny story. I laughed heartily and was still laughing
when the waitress came by with our plates.

As she walked away, we bowed our heads
and Steve began to give thanks for our food.
But then he remembered the story he had
just told and began laughing again. Of course I
laughed with him. But instead of being dis-
tracted by the humor, Steve chose to let God
in on the hilarity. He thanked God for the
funny happenings in our lives that bring us
delight and joy.

I must admit, it felt a bit strange to laugh

during prayer. I had seldom, if ever, done that before. But it felt good to laugh with a dear Christian friend and with God Himself. Were we being disrespectful to laugh during prayer? I don't think so. In a way, it might have been more disrespectful *not* to laugh with God.

Say you walked into a room where your friends were laughing, but they saw you and instantly stopped. How would you feel? "What's so funny?" you ask. "Oh, nothing," they reply, putting on their straightest faces. "You wouldn't get it."

You feel left out! You feel insulted! They must think you have no sense of humor. Well, God must feel that way when we leave our laughter at the door of the church. Why can't we let Him in on the things we enjoy?

Awkward Moments

In a church I pastored years ago, there was a young man named Zack who had virtually no religious background. No one had ever taught him how to pray in any special "holy" way, so he just talked to God as he might talk to you or me.

"Hi, God," he prayed one morning in Sunday School, and then he began to laugh. It was a simple, honest laugh, but the rest of the class seemed to tense up. They felt awkward about Zack's casual praying. "Man, I had a good time last night," Zack continued. "These new friends at my Bible study are great. Mark and Jeff told the funniest story. . . . I'm still laughing. I'm sure glad Bible study is such a fun time. Thanks, Lord!"

Several other short prayers—much more sedate—were offered, but Zack's is the only one I still remember. No one had taught him *not* to laugh with God, and so he did. It was a natural and honest and joyful expression of how he felt. And what's wrong with that?

If you have the image of a "no-nonsense God," you may be in shock over these stories, just as Zack's classmates felt awkward about his attitude. "Laughing in prayer? Whatever happened to 'Hallowed be Thy name'?"

Certainly there is a time to stand in awe of God's holiness and majesty, but the Scriptures also call us to delight in His presence. Of course we would never laugh *at* God or make fun of Him, but why shouldn't we treat Him as a friend we enjoy?

"Let Israel rejoice in their Maker," the psalmist sings. "Let the people of Zion be glad in their King. . . . For the Lord takes delight in His people" (Ps. 149:2-4).

This is not a picture of a "no-nonsense God" cracking a whip over us as we do His bidding. It's a picture of a God of joy, one who takes delight in us as we take delight in Him. As we glance over the history of Israel—yes, we see God crackling thunder from Sinai—but we also see *parties*, lots of them. Passover, Pentecost, Harvest—the Israelites were called to get together frequently and feast together in God's honor. Yes, God wanted them to live holy and faithful lives, but He also wanted them to celebrate His presence! David exulted, "I rejoiced with those who said to me, 'Let us go to the house of the Lord' " (Ps. 122:1). Why would he rejoice? Maybe he had fun in the Lord's house.

Is that possible? Can we worship with hilarity? Can we laugh with reverence? I certainly hope so. "Joy" is listed second among the fruit of the Spirit in Galatians 5:22. Many interpreters have rushed to explain this joy as a deep-seated contentment, not a constant comedy act. Maybe that's true, but surely it carves a place in our lives for laughter, fun, and delight.

As my friend David Mains has said, "Sometimes in the modern church we get more serious about the Lord than we should. That's not to say we should take Him lightly; rather, we should take Him *with delight*" (David R. Mains with Laurie Mains, *Putting God in His Place: Making Sure He Receives the Worship He Deserves* (StarSong Publishing, 1994).

The Twinkle in Jesus' Eye

You can't read the Gospels without encountering the humor of Jesus. His teaching often included funny stories, absurd word pictures, and sharp witticisms. Modern scholars may have reduced the parables to grim object lessons, but surely Jesus told these stories with a smile and a twinkle in His eye. The rich man who vowed to tear down his barns and build bigger barns is a tragicomic figure if ever there was one, and there is deep irony in the story of the servant who was forgiven a debt of millions and then turned around and demanded payment of a few bucks from someone else. Jesus spoke at length about the overly pious leaders, how they polished their cups carefully on the outside, but neglected to clean the inside. He depicted them straining their drinks to eliminate the tiny gnats, but ignoring the big hairy camels they were swallowing! They were blind people leading blind people, Jesus said, and both would fall into a ditch. This is slapstick material! And isn't there a sense of "Gotcha!" as Jesus says, "Give Caesar what is Caesar's, but give God what is God's"?

Seeing the humor in these scenes does not take anything away from their essential truth or their power to teach us. As any schoolteacher will tell you, humor helps make material user-friendly. Students' minds are more fertile when they are tilled with laughter.

But not only did Jesus *say funny things,* He also loved to *go to parties.* You can hardly turn a page in the Gospels without seeing Jesus at some social event. He invites Levi the tax collector (aka Matthew) to become His disciple, and the next thing you know, Levi's throwing a "great banquet for Jesus at his house, and a large crowd of tax collectors and others were eating with them" (Luke 5:29). The religious leaders even criticized Jesus for hanging out with such sinners, but Jesus was not dissuaded.

Encountering another tax collector, Zaccheus, Jesus invited Himself to the man's house for dinner, and Zaccheus obliged by throwing another party. Once Jesus quoted some of the criticisms that had been leveled at Him: "Here is a glutton and a drunkard, a friend of tax collectors and sinners" (Matt. 11:19). Of course these charges were overdone—Jesus did not commit the sins of gluttony or drunkenness—but it's clear that Jesus liked to have a good time.

I have the feeling that, if Jesus walked in our society today, He would receive the same criticism from some Christians I know. For "no-nonsense" believers, Jesus would be having entirely too much fun.

Once Jesus was visiting His friends Mary and Martha in Bethany. Martha was scurrying around, playing hostess for Jesus and His disciples, while Mary sat at Jesus' feet. After a while, Martha complained that Mary was shirking the work that had to be done. "Tell her to help me!" she requested.

Whenever I've heard this story taught or preached, I've pictured a rather serious scene—Mary with the other disciples in rapt attention as Jesus explained the Hebrew

Scriptures. But now that I think about it, the whole scene was probably much lighter. The Bible says Mary was "listening to what [Jesus] said." But what sort of thing did Jesus say? As we have seen, Jesus' teaching was often fun and funny. It's likely that Mary and the disciples were laughing as Jesus spun out a new parable. Did Martha hear their laughter from the kitchen? Was that what brought her out in a tirade?

We don't know. But we know how Jesus responded: "Martha, Martha," He began. You can almost hear Him trying to slow her down. "You are worried and upset about many things, but only one thing is needed. Mary has chosen what is better and it will not be taken away from her" (Luke 10:41-42).

I see "no-nonsense" Christians today scurrying around like Martha, frantically trying to *get the job done.* Yes, they're doing some very important things, but they can become "worried and upset." They can focus so much on the *task* that they forget the *relationship.* That's what Mary chose — a joy-filled relationship with Christ. That's "what is better" — being with Jesus, learning and laughing with Him.

His Banqueting Table

I have a cherished memory of children in Vacation Bible School singing songs of praise from the bottom of their hearts and at the top of their voices. "He lifts me to His banqueting table," they sang in one favorite chorus. "His banner over me is love." Their faces were aglow as the guitarist pounded out the chords in an upbeat tempo. This was a room filled with energy. This was *fun*.

Too many of those children have learned the wrong lesson as they have grown up. They have learned that fun is fine when you're trying to keep a cadre of kids occupied for two weeks each summer, but the real stuff of Christianity is dead serious. The songs they sing in *adult* church are much slower and softer. Try to sing those at the top of your voice, and you'll get a pew-full of nasty glares, and perhaps a quick slap from your mom.

Adult church is serious, and meditative, and boring. If things aren't boring enough, people start to complain. "Pastor, your sermon was entirely too interesting last week. See that it doesn't happen again."

There is no running in church. There is no shouting in church, except when Mr. Wilson barks "Amen" after the organ offertory. There is no clapping in church. There is no loud dumping of your pennies into the offering plate. Children learn these things.

And we wonder why "Let us go to the house of the Lord" is met with grumbling, not with the psalmist's rejoicing.

I hope your church is not like the picture I've just painted. I hope your services are full of joy as well as reverence, excitement as well as reflection. I hope your children are learning that a relationship with God can make their lives more fascinating than Saturday morning TV.

"He lifts me to his banqueting table. His banner over me is love." I can still hear that chorus, drawn from the lush love lyrics of the Song of Songs (2:4). So let's feast together with our Lord. Let's unfurl those banners that display just how much we love Him "because He first loved us."

This is the major scriptural image for our relationship with God—not a lecture hall, but a banquet hall; not a term paper due next Friday, but a dinner party this Sunday.

Every time we celebrate the Lord's Supper, we are feasting with Him. For the moment, put down your theological wranglings over exactly when and how the bread *is* the body of Christ—just come and dine. Jesus Christ is present with us, in some way, we all agree. He is the host of this banquet, and He is the honored guest. He has sent His servants out to the "highways and byways" to bring us in as guests, and here we are.

It is a time of remembrance, as we ponder the deep mysteries of Christ's sacrificial death on our behalf. But it is also a time of joy, as we revel in the benefits of that death. He has won our salvation. Let us sing Hallelujah. We dine in thanksgiving for what He has done.

And we look forward to another meal, at the end of time. "Blessed are those who are invited to the wedding supper of the Lamb," says the Book of Revelation (19:9). When the final victory is won, Christ the sacrificial Lamb will take the church as His holy bride.

Will that be a party, or what?

Questions for Reflection and Discussion

Chapters 5–6

1. Have you ever felt so pressured into "doing good things" that you lost the joy of serving? In this sense, is God a taskmaster? Why or why not?

2. How would you describe the delight or the "fun factor" that can be found in serving the Lord?

3. React to this statement: "I want to burn out for the Lord." What words of caution might we need here?

4. How do we bring balance to our Christian lives and service? What are God's expectations related to work and play?

5. If someone said, "Let's stop having fun now; it's time be spiritual," what would be your response? Why?

6. Have you ever thought of God as having the capacity to laugh? Can you see Jesus at a party today?

7. Can we laugh with reverence? When? How?

8. Where would we find Jesus ministering in today's society?

9. Should we ever think of worship as fun? Why or why not?

Chapter Seven

THE
TIGER

God as Abusive Parent

The young missionary couple was preparing to return to their Third World ministry. As we shared dinner together, I asked them about their plans, their hopes, and how our church and I could pray for them.

"You may always pray for our safety," the young wife said.

"And pray that we can teach and preach with clarity," the husband added. "There is so much superstition among the people we serve—so much fear. Pray that we can make clear the Gospel of Jesus."

He went on to speak of the widespread superstitious practices that he and other missionaries had to deal with. Pagan animism was prevalent in the land where they served, but there was another odd religion as well—a mixture of Christian beliefs and magic. Unlike

Americans, the people in this land were fascinated by spiritual things and eager to learn about God, but they were controlled by deep-seated fears. These fears had been taught to them from childhood and had become an integral part of their everyday lives.

It was very hard for them to understand that God loved them, that He wanted a relationship with them. They treated God as a ferocious tiger. If you do the right things, maybe he'll do tricks for you, but you never know when he'll attack. Even when they accepted some of the teachings of Christianity, they still mixed them with their long-held belief in magic. Superstition is based on power, not love. You fear the supernatural powers and so you arm yourself with spiritual power (or you try to) through magic or ritual.

"God Will Get You"

It is easy for us to relegate superstition to Third World cultures, but it is more common than we think, even in our own culture. Of course there are the "silly" things like not stepping on a crack in the sidewalk or a ballplayer not shaving until the team wins. But I'm talking about more serious fears.

In my years of counseling, I have met many who seemed plagued by fears of the supernatural. In some cases they had dabbled with the occult and now were terrified of the power of evil spirits. In other cases, they just feared the unpredictable wrath of God. They saw God as harsh, vindictive, and judgmental, and they tiptoed through life, so as not to disturb the Tiger. Some of these people observed practices and rituals designed to get them on God's "good side," but they never knew when He would strike out in judgment.

Even Christians sometimes mingle their faith with superstition:

"If you skip church on Sunday, bad things will happen that week."

"If you touch this prayer-cloth, God will heal your diseases."

"If you ignore this program's appeal for funds, God will bring financial disaster upon you."

The language may sound Christian, but there's also a deep belief in the fearsome power of a capricious God, whom we can try to control through our actions.

A friend of mine tells of his sixth-grade teacher, who often quoted one Scripture verse: "Be sure that your sin will find you out" (Num. 32:23). It was the only verse he ever quoted, maybe the only one he knew, but he used it effectively. If someone had stolen the teacher's favorite pen, or scribbled obscenities on the blackboard, or thrown Janie's hat out the window, this teacher would use that verse to try to get a confession. My friend says he was always a good kid—he was never the culprit—but that verse still struck fear into his heart. He was sure that God was tallying up every hidden misdeed, and that someday he'd be run over by a truck.

It's this message—"God will get you"— that runs repeatedly in the minds of many people in this world. They fear an abusive God, one who will punish them without warning for unspecified sins. A personal relationship with such a God would be dangerous, if it were possible at all.

"He Don't Care"

Michael first came to our church in 1980. Just dismissed from an alcohol and drug detoxification center, he was groping to find a new life. He was, by his own admission, a drunk. A very talented guitarist, he had spent sixteen years as a rock-and-roll singer in local bars and nightclubs. His lifestyle had taken a toll— physically, mentally, and emotionally. His vocabulary was laced with vulgarity and, even after coming to church, he was hard-pressed to control his tongue. Profanity would pop out in reaction to most any stressful incident or unexpected inconvenience.

Early in Michael's new attempt toward rehabilitation, his sister-in-law had invited him to our church. He agreed to come on a Sunday evening. It would be a new experience for Michael, both frightening and revealing. He had not attended a church service in many years, had not prayed or read the Bible and, in fact, claimed to be an atheist. Coming to church that evening, Michael was extremely apprehensive; he wasn't sure what to expect.

My sermon that evening was entitled "Love Is Something That You Do." In the message I spoke of God's love, of the Incarnation, and God's grace. I emphasized that Jesus had commanded us to love one another. Michael was amazed. In my office a couple of days later he spoke of my sermon, the first he had ever remembered really hearing.

"That was some talk you gave, Preacher," he said. From there, he described what he had always believed about churches, about Christian people, and especially about God. None of it was positive.

Michael's concept of God was obvious. From early childhood he had viewed God as an awesome and angry God. In animated words punctuated with profanity, he expressed his thoughts.

"First of all," he began, "if there is a God, He's way out there somewhere and He sure don't care what's going on down here. And if He did pay attention, He'd be mean. I can see Him up there watching us. You get out of line and He's going to hurt you, just reach down and get you whenever He wants."

Michael was getting excited as he described his view of God. In his face I saw anger mixed with fear. He continued, "When I think of all that I have done—liquor and drugs and bars, women, carousing around, I ain't got a chance. I can't believe God's ever going to love me. Man, I'm scared to even think about what He might do to me."

It would be many months, even years before Michael's fear of God would change from dread and anxiety to a fear equated with awe and reverence. As the church became more and more of Michael's life, he grew in his appreciation of the Christian life. He was regular in services and Bible study, prayed constantly, and memorized Scripture. Before long he was working in a local Christian bookstore. There he became intimately acquainted with a broad scope of Christian literature and music.

Michael also grew in understanding of himself. One day he told me of his inordinate fear of God, relating his view of God to his relationship to his dad.

"My dad," he explained, "was a no-nonsense man. Sometimes he seemed benevolent, touching on affectionate. Like, he'd take us for ice cream. But, man, he was unpredictable. He would hit me without warning. Someone else could do a job perfectly, but I couldn't do anything right. I'd get punished without reason. I had an overpowering fear of the man, of what might come next."

Now he spoke in more subdued terms: "When you first talked about our Heavenly Father, my mind shut down. If God was like a father, I wanted nothing to do with Him."

"What changed?" I asked.

"Oh, as I learned more about the Bible, and as I learned to pray, and the more I was with God's people in worship, I came to know God's loving presence. Now fearful situations only make His presence seem more real. I know God is with me to protect me."

For Michael, God had become the kind of father he never had. This man was stunned by the message of God's love, and by the demonstration of love from God's people. He was able to draw a whole new picture of God, different from the image of the harsh Judge his mind had held earlier.

Many people never get to that point. They find it much harder to shake that idea of God as an abusive father. This is especially difficult when their own fathers were abusive. We blithely quote Psalm 103:13 — "As a father has compassion on his children, so the Lord has compassion on those who fear Him," and they say, "Huh? What? That's not like any father I know." We have to use different images for God, or we have to redefine fatherhood in terms of God's amazing love.

When Christians Fear God's Abuse

You might think that the view of God as an abusive father would remain outside the church. Doesn't a person have to accept God's love in order to become a Christian? Isn't there a relationship started that would overcome the fear of abuse?

Yes and no. With their conversion, many people come close enough to God to join the family, but those old ideas can still haunt them. Even if they don't fear eternal damnation anymore, they may fear what God might do to make their earthly lives miserable.

Losing Out with God

Some Christians are afraid God will disown them. They are afraid they will commit some unforgivable sin and their names will be crossed out of the Lamb's Book of Life. These are the people who keep going forward at every altar call, just to make sure it "takes."

Some have the idea that, if they were to die with some unknown, unconfessed sin in their heart, they would not go to heaven. Michael, from the story above, mentioned that he sometimes worries that he might be committing a sin when Jesus returns. That keeps him from committing many sins, which is good, but the fear still haunts him.

For some, this fear arises at the Lord's Supper when the congregation is warned against "drinking the cup of the Lord unworthily." Many tender souls worry that there may be some hidden sin that will cause them to "eat and drink damnation to themselves" (see 1 Cor. 11:17-34).

When you consider these examples, you see that they all have to do with our works, not God's grace. *I* have to get 'fessed up. *I* have to scour my soul to see if there's any sin there. *I* have to live a perfect life so that there will be no outstanding sins when I die. But that goes against the grain of Scripture. While "faith without deeds is dead" (James 2:26), the Bible repeatedly reminds us that *God's grace* saves us, not our deeds.

In Matthew 5:48, Jesus teaches, "Be perfect, therefore, as your Heavenly Father is perfect," but here the idea is not that we live perfect lives. We all have faults—physical, mental, emotional, even spiritual—but we can live without blame. Why? Again, because we are saved by grace. God sees us through Christ. Further, we should remember to live *intentionally.* That is, we get up every morning intending to live each moment for Christ. We are called to righteousness and holiness, a life made possible only by the empowering presence of God's Holy Spirit. Paul said, "I have been crucified with Christ, and I no longer live, but Christ lives in me" (Gal. 2:20)—and that makes all the difference. Our relationship with God becomes a two-way street. As we live intentionally for Christ, no one can pluck us from the hand of God. And as Paul assures us, nothing "will be able to separate us from the love of God" (Rom. 8:39).

Yet many superstitious tendencies have crept into our religion. We keep looking for ways to manipulate the power of God, or ways that we might run afoul of it.

The "unforgivable sin" that Jesus mentioned (Matt. 12:31-32) is the sin of rejecting the Holy Spirit's testimony about Jesus. For the Christian who has an ongoing relationship with Christ, who has thus *accepted* the Spirit's testimony, it would be impossible to commit this sin.

The Scriptures on the Lord's Supper refer to a situation in Corinth where people were coming together for all the wrong reasons—pride, factionalism, gluttony. The call to "examine yourselves" is a valuable one, but the intention is: "Examine why you're here at the Lord's table." These Corinthians were missing out on the true nature of the body of Christ. The word for "damnation" (*krima*) is better translated "judgment" or "punishment." Paul indicates that there was physical sickness that resulted from the false motives (and perhaps from their gluttony).

There's an issue here that not all churches agree on. Can we live with the assurance of our salvation? Certainly we can. The weight of Scripture supports this conclusion. "If we confess our sins, He is faithful and just and will forgive us our sins and purify us from all unrighteousness" (1 John 1:9). It's as if the chalkboard record of our sins has been wiped clean with a wet cloth. All gone. As we become aware of "missing the mark," sinning intentionally or otherwise, we should confess it, stay close to God, and keep growing in our faith—but we need not fear the fires of hell. Let me assure those tender souls who may be reading this that we *can* live with the assurance of our salvation.

This Is Too Good

I spoke with a woman who admitted that she had a good life. She had a loving husband, two darling children, a comfortable house, and a decent business. "This is too good," she told me. "I keep waiting for something to go wrong. God can't let me have it this good. Eventually He has to make me suffer."

She came from a religious background where there was a heavy emphasis on working for your salvation—well, working for everything. God rewarded those who worked hard for Him and punished those who did not. Now she feels as if she's being rewarded, but she's not sure what she did to deserve it. It's like finding a bag of money that was dropped from a Brink's truck. Don't spend too much, because they will probably find you, and you'll have to pay it all back.

This woman fears that her life will all even out eventually—she *will* have to suffer for all this—and so she can't bring herself to enjoy her life too much right now.

My advice to this woman, and others like her, is simple. Don't worry. Do all you can to share your blessings with others—but *enjoy what God gives you.* Someday He may call you to suffer for Him. He may bring trials your way, but He will also give you the strength to deal with those trials. And you will find joy even in those difficult times. So find the joy here too.

My Will vs. God's

As a girl at a church missions conference, Charity felt called to India as a missionary. Growing up, she made her plans, learning as much as she could about that area. She felt it was what God wanted her to do, and she didn't question it. At least not until she was older.

The fact is that she was terrified of India. The more she learned about it, the more afraid she became. She felt she was not cut out for missions there. In addition, some health problems would make it difficult for her to be away from the U.S. Still, she harked back to that missions conference — God wanted her in India . . . didn't He?

In college, she found that she had some acting ability. She did well in college productions and worked briefly with a church drama group. This was something she thoroughly enjoyed, but when the opportunity arose for her to join a touring Christian drama group, she hesitated. It was perfect for her, a way to use her God-given talents in His service, but there was one problem — she felt she wanted it too much.

Her Christian life had always been a battle of wills. Hers and God's. She had learned to submit her will to the will of God. Whenever she wanted something, she was sure that God wanted something else. If she was happy about anything, it must be that she was displeasing God.

So when the wonderful opportunity arose to minister through drama, it was, frankly, too wonderful. She had to give it up in order to do what God wanted. The idea that God might want something that would make her happy too never really registered with her. God was "abusive" in the sense that His will was always opposed to hers. As she saw it, He couldn't stand to see her happy.

I will not deny that there is often a struggle of wills in Christian living. We do need to learn to submit to God's way. But I also know that God wants what is best for us, and that is often (not always) something that makes us feel happy, abundant, fulfilled. "Delight yourself in the Lord," the psalmist says, "and He will give you the desires of your heart" (Ps. 37:4). There's some tautology in that—we learn to delight in what God wants—but it still speaks of our desire being one with God's, not opposed to it.

Don't Send Me to Siberia

When I was a teenager in our church youth group, becoming a Christian automatically meant you considered some form of ministry. I dreaded that. I did not want to "marry, bury, baptize, preach, and pray"! I intended to be a physician. It was what my family expected, and what I had planned for. Still, a very persistent pastor's wife would point her finger in my face and say, "Now David, don't you stoop to be a doctor if God wants you to be a minister." The words irritated me. They only fed my fear.

This is very similar to the battle of wills I just spoke about. I was held back in my relationship with God for a while because I couldn't trust Him to do what was best with my life. Become a Christian and God takes over—no more doing what you want to do. I didn't want to give up my dream of medical school. I also didn't want to give up certain friends and activities that didn't fit our church's standards for the Christian life.

Fortunately, I got past that. I eventually let God lead me—surprise!—into the ministry. But I've talked with several believers who have had similar hesitations.

"I was afraid He would send me as a missionary to Siberia," said one man.

Another woman confided, "I thought I'd have to give up all the fun things in my life. The woman who led me to Christ didn't do much except meditate on the Lord, and that seemed really boring to me. I was really afraid I'd have to become like her."

God does make changes in people's lives, but He changes our hearts too. I believe I have found more fulfillment in my various ministries than I ever would have had as a doctor.

We learn to enjoy what He wants for us.

Chapter Eight

THE SHEPHERD

God Wants What's Best for Us

Palm Sunday 1994. A tornado rips through a church in Piedmont, Alabama, during a worship service, interrupting a children's drama. At least eighteen worshipers were killed, including six children. Among them was the pastor's five-year-old daughter.

Why?

The evening news has been filled with bloodshed in Eastern Europe, Africa, and our own city streets. A recent movie, *Schindler's List,* documented the ferocity of the Holocaust that killed 6 million Jews. Even weather reports in recent years have been dotted with tragedy—floods in the Midwest, hurricanes in the Southeast, fires and earthquakes in California. But the news on Palm Sunday was starkly upsetting. A church. A worship service. A minister. A little girl.

How could God let this happen?

I don't have easy answers for you. The bloodshed of war and crime can at least be explained as human waywardness, but who's to blame for a tornado? As any insurance company will tell you, it's an "act of God."

Some people would take this as evidence to support their claim that God is abusive. They recite a litany of natural disasters and proclaim, "If there were truly a loving God, He wouldn't let this happen."

Some have been victimized themselves — by illness, by natural events, or by other humans — and they nurse a grudge against this "hateful" God. They feel used and abused by the powers that be, and they turn away.

I know a woman whose husband left her last year. She is a Christian and struggling to hold onto her faith, but this is tough to deal with. Her husband is a Christian too (or so he claims), but now she's suffering while he's living happily with another woman. It's not fair! Shouldn't God punish him for treating her so miserably? And why is He allowing her to suffer so much?

If God treats the people who *love* Him like this, what kind of God is He? With friends like Him, who needs enemies? Please forgive the bluntness, but this is the quandary of those who feel abused by events that God has caused, or at least allowed. Somewhere inside their souls, they may still believe that God cares for them, but He sure has a funny way of showing it. Why doesn't the tornado veer away from the church? Why doesn't the philandering husband go bankrupt?

We aren't the first to question God's tactics. The psalmists on several occasions bemoaned the prosperity of the wicked and the suffering of the righteous. It seemed that God was letting the wicked get away with murder, and that just wasn't fair. "Awake, O Lord!" cried the sons of Korah. "Why do You sleep? Rouse Yourself! Do not reject us forever. Why do You hide Your face and forget our misery and oppression?" (Ps. 44:23-24)

That whole psalm proclaims the innocence of God's people and complains about how they've been treated. Yet the final verse still reaches out to the Lord: "Rise up and help us; redeem us because of Your unfailing love" (v. 26).

Unfailing love? Haven't they just been charging God with miserable *failure*? Yes, but when all is said and done, they rest on His unfailing love. Maybe there's a loophole. Maybe it's their understanding that has failed somehow. Maybe God is still loving in spite of these tragedies. That is the response of faith in the midst of crisis.

The Big Picture
So how can we explain it when God seems to be abusive? Ask your dentist.

Once, as I sat in the dentist's chair, I asked,

"Is this going to hurt?" Silly question, right?

But my friend the dentist had a wise answer. "Yes, I will hurt you," he said, "but I will not harm you." There would be pain (and there was!), but the procedure was being done for my overall good.

A person can save himself a good deal of pain if he never goes to the dentist—but it will cost him a lot of pain later on. In the big picture, the dental work is worth it.

So it is in our lives. There may be something painful going on now, but it may be saving us from future disaster, or ensuring us future blessing. My coauthor, Randy Petersen, tells of the pain of losing his job eight years ago. The newsletters he was editing had become unprofitable, and he had to be laid off. In the next six months, he interviewed for a number of editorial positions, but just missed being selected. He was taking freelance jobs to make ends meet, but he was still underemployed, with no assurances for the future. On top of all that, he learned that he had to move out of his apartment. It wasn't easy finding a new apartment when he had no steady employer to give as a reference.

There was one rejection that was especially troubling. A Christian magazine needed an editor, and Randy was perfectly suited for the job. He made it to the short list of three applicants, but someone else got the job, leaving Randy to wonder if he'd ever find his place.

Meanwhile, the freelance jobs kept coming. Within the next six months, he was fully employed by various clients as a freelance writer and editor. He was doing something he had always dreamed of doing, and loving it.

There were moments in that bleak period when Randy felt used and abused by God. He had started his career in the low-paying world of Christian journalism, and how had God rewarded him? With unemployment. But in the big picture, the curse became a blessing. Without that layoff, without those rejections, Randy wouldn't be writing this book today.

Incidentally, that Christian magazine that *almost* hired Randy had financial difficulties and went out of business a year later. Maybe God really did know what He was doing. It would have been even more difficult for Randy to get that job and then lose it a year later. It's amazing how wise God looks in the rearview mirror.

Master Teacher

God also may seem to be abusing us when He is teaching us important lessons. If a parent never allows a child to fail on his own, the child will not learn much. When a toddler learns to walk, the parent holds her hands to prevent a nasty fall. But soon the parent must let go. The toddler will fall on her face a few times—but that's how people learn to walk!

In one baseball movie, a brash young pitcher keeps shaking off the signs from his older, wiser catcher. The catcher runs out to the mound to confer, and the pitcher says he wants to throw a fastball. "Throw a curve," the catcher advises. "He'll kill your fastball." But the hotshot hurler insists.

The catcher goes back to the plate and tells the batter a fastball is coming. Sure enough, the batter hits a long home run.

That wise old catcher hurt the pitcher by letting the batter hit a home run. But he also taught the pitcher a valuable lesson: "Don't think you know it all. Listen to the wise advice of others."

In the same way, God uses difficult times to teach us important lessons. It may seem that He is punishing us, but he has our best interests at heart.

I heard of one newly founded church that had a slew of difficulties in its first year. They planned to start their services in April, and planned a huge phone campaign to launch it. But the school building where they were supposed to meet wasn't available until November. They had to postpone.

When they did start, there were regular problems with the sound system. The synthesizer went dead. The Communion table fell down. Key people got ministries started, but then had to leave the area.

People with an "abusive-parent" view of God might say that He was torturing these people. But this church had quite a different view. At each step of the way, they learned this lesson: "We are not in control; God is. This is *His* church. Things never turn out the way we plan; they turn out *better*." And now, four years later, despite some nervous moments along the way, the church includes about 400 people whose lives are being touched and changed by God's power. Their plans still go awry from time to time, but they've been learning—it's God's church; He has that prerogative.

Needs, Not Wants

Children can be very convincing when they throw tantrums. When you see a parent with a screaming child, sometimes it's easy to side with the kid. "I want some ice cream! Just a little ice cream! Pleeeeeeease!"

Come on, Mom. What can it hurt?

But Mom knows that a little ice cream will spoil that kid's dinner. He won't eat the carrots that he needs to eat in order to grow strong. If children got everything they asked for, they would only hurt themselves. They need wise parents who will distinguish wants from needs.

Sometimes we can throw tantrums with God. "Please, God, I need this job/spouse/car. Pleeeeeeease!" When He doesn't give us what we want, we get mad. "After all I've done for You, You could at least give me this! I deserve this! I thought You loved me!"

God doesn't fall for that blackmail. Well,

sometimes, I think, He gives us what we want even if it's bad for us, in order to teach us to rely on Him. One young man told me he prayed for a whole year that a particular girl would become his girlfriend. Finally she did, and four months later he was praying to get out of the relationship gracefully. But, apart from those exceptions, God usually gives us our daily *bread,* not our daily *chocolate cake.*

Hosea, Can You See?

The Prophet Hosea had reason to feel abused by God. He was told to marry a prostitute, as an object lesson of God's relationship with His people: "Go, take to yourself an adulterous wife and children of unfaithfulness, because the land is guilty of the vilest adultery in departing from the Lord" (Hosea 1:2).

(It may be that his wife was not a prostitute until after he married her, and that Hosea is assuming God's foreknowledge as he describes the scene. That is, he may be saying, "God called me to marry this woman, knowing full well that she would be unfaithful.")

As you might expect, the relationship caused Hosea great pain. We get glimpses of his situation in the first three chapters of his book, though it's not always clear which are his feelings and which are God's. Yet we know that his wife was unfaithful, and probably left him, even though he had provided well for her and her two illegitimate children.

But God wanted Hosea to take her back. "The Lord said to me, 'Go, show your love to your wife again, though she is loved by another and is an adulteress. Love her as the Lord loves the Israelites, though they turn to other gods and love the sacred raisin cakes.' So I bought her for fifteen shekels of silver and about a homer and a lethek of barley. Then I told her, 'You are to live with me many days; you must not be a prostitute or be intimate with any man, and I will live with you' " (3:1-3).

That's right. Hosea had to buy his own wife back (presumably from the brothel). This too was a picture of God's relationship with Israel—redeeming her and bringing her back from captivity, despite her idolatry.

In the rest of this book, God speaks directly to His people Israel. He speaks of His unrequited love, He threatens punishment, and He complains about being rejected.

When Israel was a child, I loved him, and out of Egypt I called my son. But the more I called Israel, the further they went from Me. They sacrificed to the Baals and they burned incense to images. It was I who taught Ephraim to walk, taking them by the arms; but they did not realize it was I who healed them (11:1-3).

Now God is the scorned parent. But with His unfailing love, He concludes, "How can I give you up, Ephraim? How can I hand you over, Israel? . . . My heart is changed within Me; all My compassion is aroused" (v. 8).

God loves and suffers and punishes and redeems. Ironically, God is saying many of the same things to Israel that the psalmist says in Psalm 44 and elsewhere. "I've been good to you! Why do you turn away?" God himself suffers injustice too.

But what about Hosea? Here's a prophet of God, obedient to the last crazy detail. Why does God mess up his life like this? Anyone who has suffered a romantic breakup knows the pain Hosea must have gone through—yet God specifically ordered him to go through this. Wasn't God being abusive? Wasn't He using Hosea as a pawn in His plans? Sure, He had a great object lesson to teach Israel, a morality play performed in real life on the streets and alleys of Samaria, but was He being fair to the Prophet Hosea?

Yes, Hosea was used, but in the same way that a ballplayer is "used" by a coach to play the game they both love. "I need a squeeze bunt here, Slugger."

"Sure thing, coach."

They're in it together; they do what it takes.

So Hosea had a chance to participate in a drama written by God Himself. He was offered the privilege of feeling God's feelings. He could suffer with God, and maybe understand God's heart in a way that no one else ever would. He could help bring his nation back to God.

Hosea ends his book with a curious maxim: "Who is wise? He will realize these things. Who is discerning? He will understand them. The ways of the Lord are right; the righteous walk in them, but the rebellious stumble in them" (14:9).

When the Lord's ways seem abusive, you have two choices—righteous or rebellious. You can turn away, even run away, embittered by the Lord's apparent lack of love. That's the "rebellious" approach, and you will "stumble." Or you can end up where the psalmist does, with the "unfailing love of God." We cannot understand it all, but we can follow faithfully.

Slaves and Sons

We come back to *relationship*. In the Book of Hosea, God sounds like a smitten lover or a doting mother. He just can't get Israel out of His mind! He hates what they've done, but He loves them, He really loves them.

Outside of a relationship with God, it makes some sense to be afraid of Him. He is awesome. He has the power of the universe in His hands, and He does things with it that we don't understand. If we are merely servants in His household, we might cower in terror. But we have a relationship with our Lord.

"For you did not receive a spirit of slavery

to fall back into fear," Paul writes, "but you have received a spirit of adoption. When we cry, '*Abba*, Father!' it is that very Spirit bearing witness with our spirit that we are children of God" (Rom. 8:15-16, NRSVB).

We are in the family! We are like children crawling up on Daddy's lap. We put our lives in His hands, trusting that our *Abba* wants what is best for us.

Later, the same chapter assures us that "in all things God works for the good of those who love Him, who have been called according to His purpose" (v. 28). *His purpose*—there's the big picture. He may be using us, but for some glorious result. "I consider that our present sufferings are not worth comparing with the glory that will be revealed in us" (v. 18).

But is Paul dealing honestly with the questions? That's an awfully easy answer for the tough questions of Hosea, Job, Jeremiah, and Psalm 44. But it's not that easy. Paul acknowledges human suffering and puts God *on our side*. "If God is for us, who can be against us? He who did not spare His own Son, but gave Him up for us all—how will He not also, along with Him, graciously give us all things?" (Rom. 8:31-32) As Hosea has been telling us, *God suffers too*.

But through it all, Paul says, the Lord loves us. "Who shall separate us from the love of Christ? Shall trouble or hardship or persecution or famine or nakedness or danger or sword? As it is written: 'For your sake we face death all day long; we are considered as sheep to be slaughtered' " (vv. 35-36). Paul offers a checklist as terrifying as our modern newspaper headlines. Do tornadoes and hurricanes and civil wars separate us from Christ's love? It may seem so—and, interestingly, Paul draws the "sheep to be slaughtered" quote from Psalm 44—but Paul goes on to give an emphatic answer:

> *No,* in all these things we are more than conquerors through Him who loved us. For I am convinced that neither death nor life, neither angels nor demons, neither the present nor the future, nor any powers, neither height nor depth, nor anything else in all creation, will be able to separate us from the love of God that is in Christ Jesus our Lord (Rom. 8:37-39).

The Lord's love is stronger than the disasters He allows. That may not make a lot of sense to us, but Jesus assures us that His intentions toward us are honorable. "The thief comes only to steal and kill and destroy; I have come that they may have life, and have it to the full. I am the good shepherd. The good shepherd lays down his life for the sheep" (John 10:10-11).

With a Savior like that, we need not be afraid.

Questions for Reflection and Discussion

Chapters 7–8

1. Ask yourself, "Have I ever been afraid of God or what He might do?" Was this fear related to something you had said or done? If so, what?

2. How do you react to fear? (Circle all that apply.)
   a. Accept it? Even study it? Look at its origin?
   b. Talk about it? Get counseling?
   c. Ignore it and hope it will go away?
   d. Give it to God, knowing He cares?
   e. Other _____

3. Is it OK to be afraid? Why or why not? When is fear appropriate?

4. What does it mean to be forgiven? How complete is God's forgiveness? What does Scripture say?

5. Is God's will for us ever what we want or enjoy? Explain. Why is it hard for some to trust God to do what's best for their lives?

6. Tornadoes, floods, and earthquakes are often referred to as "acts of God." Is God at fault? How do we react when bad things happen to God's people?